THE
NEW AMERICANA
COOKBOOK

A Heart-Healthy Excursion
Through Regional Cuisines

By
Sherri Eldridge

Illustrations by
Robert Groves
Nadine Pranckunas

The gratitude of the author is extended to the Maine Chapter of the American Heart Association for the guidance and information provided. For each book sold the publisher makes a contribution to the American Heart Association to further their life-preserving efforts of research and education.

The New Americana Cookbook
A Heart-Healthy Excursion Through Regional Cuisines
by Sherri Eldridge

Published by:
CNE Publications, Inc.
P.O. Box 55, Salisbury Cove, Maine 04672
(207) 288-8988

ISBN: 1-886862-06-0

First printing: March 1997
Second printing: July 1997

10 9 8 7 6 5 4 3 2

PRINTED IN THE U.S.A.
ON ACID FREE PAPER

PREFACE

One of America's great cultural pleasures is the diversity we enjoy in our regional and ethnic cuisines. Nowhere in the world do people have such a broad selection of fresh produce, meats and spices, with so many distinct local styles to savor and explore. This book is a celebration of smooth southern cooking, the lively styles of the Atlantic coast, and traditional New England fare. It reaches down to the Tex-Mex chili border, and across the wide west to wine country. And through the heartland breadbasket and Great Lakes, we are joined in the bounty and interpretation of flavors that have created *The New Americana Cookbook*.

We are benefitted today by a wealth of nutritional knowledge, which has increased our expectancy to live a long and productive life. The American Heart Association has developed guidelines to assist in the prevention of heart disease. A pleasurable diet, low in fats and meats, and high in fresh vegetables, fruits, fish and grains has also been shown to have numerous other health benefits.

These recipes have been adapted to meet the guidelines of the American Heart Association for healthy adults. Although all recipes are reduced in fat and cholesterol, those such as chocolate desserts should not be eaten every day, but might be enjoyed once or twice a week. A heart-healthy diet includes diverse and good-tasting dishes that are reasonably low in fat, served in average size proportions, employing common sense meal plans, and regular exercise.

The Hints and References section has specific guidelines for a heart-healthy diet. Also shown is data on the fats and cholesterol found in oils. Although the sodium and sugars in these recipes has been reduced or removed, people on strict diets should adapt recipes to their individual needs.

Please take a few minutes and explore the resources in this book. It has been carefully written to offer you the best of The New Americana Cooking.

This book is dedicated to

The American Heart Association

for their unceasing efforts
of research, education and care,
aiding us in helping ourselves and those we love.

CREDITS:

Front and Back Cover Borders, and Chapter Page Borders:
Adapted from the cotton print "In the Kitchen," gratefully used as a courtesy of:
Alexander Henry Fabrics

Cover Designs, Layout and Typesetting: Sherri Eldridge

Front Cover Hillside Garden Watercolor: Robert Groves, Brooksville, Maine

Text Line Sketches: Robert Groves and Nadine Pranckunas

Support, Patience and Recipes: Bill Eldridge and Fran Goldberg

Some of the recipes used in this book have been previously published in the Coastal New England Cooking Series, by Sherri Eldridge, published by CNE Publications, Inc.

THE NEW AMERICANA COOKBOOK
CONTENTS

Breakfast
and
Fresh Fruits

THE NEW AMERICANA COOKBOOK

CONTENTS

For other breakfast foods, please refer to the chapters "Breads and Baked Goods" and "Desserts and Sweets."

THE NEW AMERICANA COOKBOOK

Whipped Apricot Creme

4 fresh apricots or
    peaches
1 cup fresh melon or
    pineapple pieces
1 banana
$1/2$ cup honey
2 cups non-fat plain
    yogurt
fresh fruit for garnish

SERVES 4

Poach apricots or peaches for 5 minutes in boiling water. Remove fruit when cool, skin and discard the pits.

Refrigerate poached fruit, melon and banana for 15-20 minutes. Put all ingredients in blender. Process until smooth. Serve in tall glasses with fresh fruit garnish.

THE NEW AMERICANA COOKBOOK

A Bowl of Ambrosia

A cheery fruit medley to brighten any cold winter morning.

3 large navel oranges
3 ripe bananas
$^{1}/_{2}$ cup fresh pineapple
     pieces, or unsweetened
     canned pineapple
$^{1}/_{4}$ cup honey or sugar
$^{3}/_{4}$ cup shredded coconut
4 tablespoons orange juice
cherries or strawberries
     for garnish (optional)

SERVES 4

Carefully peel and remove membranes from orange sections, leaving sections whole.

Cut bananas into small pieces. Combine bananas with pineapple, honey or sugar, and shredded coconut.

Arrange alternate layers of oranges and banana/pineapple mixture in individual serving dishes. Over the top of each bowl of ambrosia, sprinkle 1 tablespoon orange juice. Chill well before serving. Garnish with a cherry or strawberry.

THE NEW AMERICANA COOKBOOK

Cinnamon Baked Fruit Compote

$^1/_2$ cup red wine or water
$^2/_3$ cup honey
2 teaspoons cinnamon
1 teaspoon ground cloves
1 teaspoon lemon or lime
    juice
pinch of salt
8 apples, pears and/or
    peaches

SERVES 4-6

Preheat oven to 350°. Combine all ingredients, except fruit, in a small saucepan. Cook over medium heat for 10 minutes, stirring occasionally. Do not allow to boil.

Core fruit and cut into slices about $^1/_2$-inch thick. Spray baking pan with non-stick vegetable oil. Arrange fruit slices in pan.

Pour one-third of the spice sauce evenly over fruit slices. Place on high rack in oven. Bake 30 minutes, basting every 10 minutes with remaining spice sauce. Serve warm from the oven or chill before serving.

Honey producers are often travelling apiaries. The beekeeper with his bees and hives, travels from field to field to pollinate different crops. The delicate scent of the blossoms is then transmitted to the honey the bees produce. For example, Apple, Blueberry, Orange Blossom and Tupelo Honey are made by the bees while they pollinate these plants.

THE NEW AMERICANA COOKBOOK

Chilled Prunes in Wine

$1^1/_2$ cups dried pitted
    prunes
1 cup water
$^1/_2$ cup dry sherry or port
1 tablespoon sugar
5 thinly cut and seeded
    lemon slices
1 cup canned or fresh
    roasted chestnut
    meats (optional)

SERVES 4-6

In a medium saucepan, cover prunes with cold water and sherry or port. Bring to a boil over medium-high heat. Reduce heat and simmer 2 minutes. Mix in sugar and lemon slices, then cook another 3 minutes.

Place in covered jar and chill at least 4 hours.

Just before serving, prunes may be stuffed with chestnut meats. Serve cold or heat briefly in oven dish.

Chestnuts have relatively little fat compared to other nuts. Three ounces of roasted chestnuts contain less than 1 gram of fat, while three ounces of assorted dry roasted nuts have over 45 grams of fat!

THE NEW AMERICANA COOKBOOK

Apple-Walnut Pancakes

2 cups all-purpose flour
5 teaspoons baking
    powder
1 teaspoon salt
1 tablespoon sugar
3 eggs, separated
1 cup unsweetened
    applesauce
1 cup skim milk
3 tablespoons canola oil
$^1/_4$ cup chopped walnuts

SERVES 4

Sift together all dry ingredients. In a separate bowl beat egg yolks, applesauce, milk and oil.

Whip egg whites into soft peaks and gently fold into batter. Stir in chopped walnuts.

Spray hot griddle with non-stick oil. Pour one-third cup batter per pancake, cook on each side until light golden brown.

Apple Maple Syrup

1 cup maple syrup
3 tablespoons frozen apple
    juice concentrate
3 inch cinnamon stick

Put all ingredients together in saucepan and simmer on medium heat for 15 minutes. Remove cinnamon stick and serve warm over pancakes or waffles.

THE NEW AMERICANA COOKBOOK

Blueberry Buttermilk Pancakes

2 cups flour
2 teaspoons double-acting
   baking powder
$^1/_2$ teaspoon salt
3 tablespoons sugar
1 teaspoon baking
   soda
2 eggs
2 cups non-fat buttermilk
3 tablespoons honey
3 tablespoons canola oil

Blueberry Preparation:
1 cup blueberries, tossed
   in 3 tablespoons flour
   (if previously frozen,
   drain well before

SERVES 4

In a large bowl, sift together dry ingredients. In a separate bowl, beat eggs until fluffy, then add buttermilk, honey and oil. Make a well in dry ingredients. Slowly pour in buttermilk mixture. Stir just until combined. Lightly fold in blueberries, do not mash.

Spray preheated griddle with non-stick vegetable oil. Ladle batter onto griddle. Flip pancakes when light golden brown.

Cranberry Waffles

SERVES 4

1$\frac{1}{2}$ cups non-fat yogurt
1$\frac{1}{2}$ cups non-fat cottage
   cheese
1$\frac{1}{2}$ cups low-fat
   buttermilk
1 tablespoon vanilla
2 cups all-purpose flour
1 tablespoon baking powder
3 egg whites
$\frac{1}{2}$ cup sugar
1 cup fresh cranberries

Chop cranberries very fine, mix with sugar.

Purée yogurt and cottage cheese in blender for 4 minutes. Put in bowl and stir in buttermilk and vanilla. Sift together flour and baking powder. Whip into buttermilk mixture. Stir in sugared cranberries.

Beat egg whites to soft peaks and fold into batter. Cook in preheated waffle iron sprayed with non-stick cooking oil.

Orange Butter Sauce

3 tablespoons butter
1 cup honey
3 tablespoons orange juice
2 tablespoons finely
   grated orange rind

Cook butter, honey and orange juice over medium-high heat for 15 minutes. Stir in grated orange rind. Serve warm over waffles or pancakes.

THE NEW AMERICANA COOKBOOK

Vanilla Pecan Waffles

SERVES 4

1 cup non-fat plain
   yogurt
1 cup low-fat cottage
   cheese
2$\frac{1}{2}$ cups white flour
2 cups low-fat buttermilk
4 tablespoons sugar
1 tablespoon vanilla
   extract
5 teaspoons baking
   powder
4 egg whites
$\frac{1}{2}$ cup finely chopped
   pecans

Preheat waffle iron sprayed with non-stick vegetable oil.

Process yogurt and cottage cheese in blender until smooth. Add all other ingredients, except egg whites and pecans, blend again. Transfer to mixing bowl. In a separate bowl, beat egg whites into soft peaks, then gently fold into batter.

Ladle batter onto hot waffle iron. Sprinkle 1 tablespoon chopped pecans over each waffle before closing to cook. Spray waffle iron between waffles to assure a non-stick surface.

The pecan is native to the southeastern United States and is appreciated everywhere for its sweet richness. Pecans are easy to use and can be substituted for walnuts. Like most nuts they are high in protein, but also contain a high amount of fat. For less fat, use chopped pecans instead of whole nutmeats to spread their flavor in your baked goods.

THE NEW AMERICANA COOKBOOK

Sweet Egg Kugel

8 oz. medium uncooked
    egg noodles
$^3/_4$ cup sugar
2 tablespoons cinnamon
$^1/_2$ lb. non-fat cottage
    cheese
2 tablespoons melted
    butter
1 teaspoon vanilla extract
4 eggs
1 cup skim milk
8 oz. non-fat cream
    cheese
$1^1/_2$ cups non-fat sour
    cream

SERVES 8

Boil noodles until tender but firm to the bite. Drain. In a mixing bowl whip together $^1/_2$-cup sugar, 1 tablespoon cinnamon and remaining ingredients. Stir in noodles by hand.

Pour into casserole sprayed with non-stick oil. Mix together remaining $^1/_4$-cup sugar and 1 tablespoon cinnamon. Sprinkle over kugel.

Bake in 350° oven until browned, about 45 minutes. Serve hot.

THE NEW AMERICANA COOKBOOK

Smoked Salmon Omelette

2 oz. smoked salmon
1 teaspoon canola oil
2 large eggs
1 teaspoon water
pinch of salt
fresh ground pepper
1 tablespoon grated
    low-fat Swiss cheese

MAKES ONE OMELETTE
Multiply ingredients by number of omelettes.

Cut smoked salmon into small pieces. Sauté in oil over low heat. Keep warm.

Preheat 8-10 inch, non-stick omelette pan over high heat.

In a bowl, whisk together eggs, water, salt and pepper. Spray preheated pan with non-stick oil. Pour beaten eggs into pan ($^1/_2$ cup if you've mixed up a number of eggs). Shake and swirl pan to distribute eggs evenly. Rest pan on heat 5 seconds to firm the bottom, while spreading salmon and cheese over top.

Note: Have spatula handy to assist omelette in its formative stages. An omelette should be cooked in just 20-30 seconds!

Hold pan by its handle and jerk quickly towards you while tilting far edge over burner. Continue this process and omelette will roll over on itself. When rolled omelette forms at far end bang on handle near pan to curl edge.

THE NEW AMERICANA COOKBOOK

Texas Breakfast Burritos

1 teaspoon canola oil
1 medium onion, chopped
1 bell pepper, chopped
3 Poblano or chipotle
    chilies
5 canned plum tomatoes,
    chopped and drained
1 teaspoon lemon juice
salt and pepper to taste
8 eggs
2 tablespoons skim milk
4 large flour tortillas
$\frac{1}{2}$ cup grated low-fat
    white Cheddar cheese
3 cups cooked rice
2 cups non-fat sour cream

SERVES 4

Heat oil in pan. Add onion and bell pepper. Core, seed and scrape inside membrane from chilies, being careful not to touch your face, eyes, or children until the hot chili oils are washed from your hands. Chop chilies and add to pan. Add tomatoes and simmer 10 minutes, or until chilies are wilted. Stir in lemon juice and spices. Keep warm.

Wrap tortillas in tin foil, warm in 250° oven. Beat eggs with milk. Cook scrambled eggs in pan sprayed with non-stick oil. Layer scrambled eggs, cheese, rice, salsa and sour cream in tortillas. Roll up and serve at once.

THE NEW AMERICANA COOKBOOK

Hot Rice Pudding with Raisins

SERVES 6

4 cups skim milk
1 cup skimmed
    evaporated milk
1 cup uncooked short or
    medium-grain white
    rice
pinch of salt
1 tablespoon butter
2 teaspoons vanilla
4 tablespoons sugar
1 cup golden raisins
2 teaspoons cinnamon

Blend milks together and scald in a saucepan.

Boil water in lower pan of double boiler. Pour scalded milks into the top pan of the double boiler. Add rice and salt. Cook 1 hour over boiling water, allowing rice to soften and thicken. Stir frequently, and check to be sure water in bottom pan does not boil off.

Remove from heat while rice is still moist. Add butter, vanilla, 2 tablespoons sugar and raisins. Place warm pudding in serving dish or custard cups. Mix remaining sugar with cinnamon and sprinkle over the top.

Herbal Wreath: To a spruce or pine fir wreath, add sprigs of dried opal basil, winter savory, cinnamon sticks, anise-hyssop, bee balm, white peppermint blossoms, hydrangea and colored sage. These herbs can also be hung in small bunches from the tree, used to make a holiday center-piece or tied with ribbon on top of pomander balls.

THE NEW AMERICANA COOKBOOK

Strawberry-Rhubarb Jelly Rolls

2 cups all-purpose flour
2 teaspoons baking
powder
2 teaspoons sugar
2 cups skim milk
3 large eggs
2 tablespoons canola oil
1 cup fresh strawberries,
cleaned and cut into
small pieces
1/2 cup rhubarb stalks,
finely diced
1/2 cup sugar
1 tablespoon water
2 teaspoons cornstarch
1 teaspoon vanilla extract
1/2 teaspoon lemon juice

To Serve: Roll each jelly roll with 2 tablespoons strawberry-rhubarb sauce. If you like, dust tops with powdered sugar.

MAKES EIGHT 8-INCH JELLY ROLLS

Sift flour before measuring, then mix with baking powder and 2 teaspoons sugar. Whisk in milk, eggs and oil. Blend until perfectly smooth. Cover and rest in the refrigerator, at least 30 minutes, but preferably 1 hour.

Simmer strawberries, rhubarb and 1/2 cup sugar in covered saucepan for 15 minutes. Blend water with cornstarch, then stir into strawberries and rhubarb. Cook until thickened, then stir in vanilla and lemon juice. Keep warm on very low heat until ready to roll up in the jelly rolls.

Preheat 8-inch crepe pan over medium-high heat. Spray with 2 coats of non-stick cooking oil and quickly pour 1/3 cup batter into middle of pan, tilt to cover. After 1 minute, flip and cook 30 seconds on second side.

THE NEW AMERICANA COOKBOOK

No-Oil Granola with Fruit

2 cups quick oats
$1/_2$ cup wheat germ
$1/_2$ cup frozen apple juice
    concentrate
1 teaspoon cinnamon
1 tablespoon brown sugar
$1/_2$ cup golden raisins

SERVES 4

Preheat oven to 300°. Stir together all ingredients except raisins. Spread on cookie sheet. Stirring frequently, toast in oven for about 20 minutes, or until golden brown. Remove from oven and add raisins.

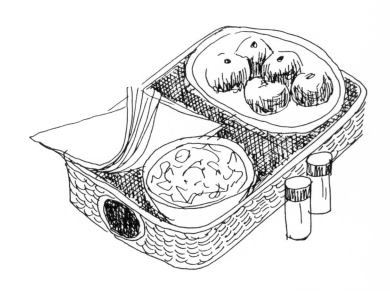

Breads
and
Baked Goods

THE NEW AMERICANA COOKBOOK

CONTENTS

Sweet baked goods are also in the chapter "Desserts and Sweets."
Spreads for bread are located in "Appetizers and Finger Food."

THE NEW AMERICANA COOKBOOK

Spiced Banana Bran Muffins

1³/₄ cups sifted all-
purpose flour
¹/₄ teaspoon salt
¹/₃ cup sugar
2 teaspoons double-acting
baking powder
1 tablespoon cinnamon
¹/₂ teaspoon ground cloves
¹/₂ cup bran flakes
2 eggs
2 tablespoons canola oil
1 teaspoon vanilla
¹/₂ cup skim milk
³/₄ cup mashed banana

MAKES 12 MUFFINS

Preheat oven to 400°. Spray muffin tins with non-stick vegetable oil.

Mix together all dry ingredients. In a separate bowl, beat eggs, then mix in remaining dry ingredients. Combine the dry and liquid mixtures with just a few swift strokes.

Fill muffin tins two-thirds full. Bake until toothpick inserted in center of muffins comes out clean, about 20-25 minutes.

Safflower oil, a healthy oil very low in saturated fat, was considered the least desirable of oils in Old World cooking. Even in India, only the poorest people benefited by using safflower oil. Historically, the healthier, natural food products have been left for the poor, as in China where only the humblest citizens once ate whole grain brown rice.

THE NEW AMERICANA COOKBOOK

Pineapple Pecan Muffins

$^1/_2$ cup non-fat plain
    yogurt
$^1/_2$ cup non-fat cottage
    cheese
3 eggs
$1^1/_2$ cups brown sugar
2 tablespoons canola oil
1 tablespoon lemon juice
2 teaspoons vanilla
    extract
3 cups all-purpose flour
1 tablespoon baking
    powder
1 cup crushed pineapple,
    drained in sieve and
    liquid pressed out
$^1/_2$ cup chopped pecans

MAKES 18 MUFFINS

Preheat oven to 350°. In large mixing bowl blend yogurt and cottage cheese with electric beater for 3 minutes. Add eggs, sugar, oil, lemon juice and vanilla. Beat well. Slowly add flour and baking powder, beat 3 minutes. By hand, gently fold in pineapple and pecans.

Lightly spray muffin tins with non-stick oil. Fill tins three-quarters full. Bake 25 minutes, or until a toothpick inserted in center of muffins comes out clean.

THE NEW AMERICANA COOKBOOK

Zucchini & Everything Nice Muffins

1 cup sugar
1 cup shredded zucchini
$^3/_4$ cup applesauce
$^1/_2$ cup raisins
2 eggs
2 teaspoons canola oil
2 cups all-purpose flour
1 teaspoon baking powder
1 teaspoon baking soda
pinch of salt
1 teaspoon allspice
1 tablespoon cinnamon

MAKES 12 MUFFINS

Preheat oven to 350°. Spray muffins tins with non-stick oil.

In a large bowl, mix sugar, shredded zucchini, applesauce, raisins, eggs and oil. In a separate bowl, combine remaining ingredients. Briefly stir flour mixture into wet ingredients, just until moistened.

Divide batter among muffin cups. Bake for 20-25 minutes or until toothpick inserted in muffins comes out clean. Immediately remove from tins and cool on wire rack.

Popovers

2 cups sifted flour
1 teaspoon salt
4 eggs
2 cups skim milk
2 tablespoons safflower
   oil

Note: Popover baking cups should be deeper than they are wide. Some custard cups can be a good substitute. Batter will be about the same consistency as thick heavy cream.

MAKES 12-16 POPOVERS

Preheat oven to 425°. If glass, cast-iron or earthenware popover pans are to be used, place in oven to heat. If using aluminum, lightly spray with non-stick vegetable oil.

In a mixing bowl, beat all ingredients with an electric beater until batter is very smooth. If popover pans were heated in oven, remove and spray with non-stick oil.

Fill cups a little less than half full. Bake for 35 minutes, without opening oven! If oven has a glass door, watch for popovers to turn a rich golden color. Best served warm with jam.

Beer Biscuits

2 cups all-purpose flour
2 teaspoons double-acting
    baking powder
2 teaspoons baking soda
8 oz. beer (1 cup)
2 tablespoons sugar

MAKES 1 DOZEN BISCUITS

Preheat oven to 375°. Spray muffin tins with non-stick oil.

Stir all ingredients together. Divide equally in tins to make 12 biscuits. Bake 15-20 minutes, or until light brown.

Beer can add a rich, yeasty flavor to many types of foods. Instead of water or broth, try beer in bean soups, fish poaching liquid, and breads. Beer is best kept cold without major temperature changes, or it will lose its flavor. The new micro-breweries that have sprung up across the country offer some great beers and interesting brewery tours.

THE NEW AMERICANA COOKBOOK

Blue Corn Tortillas

2 cups blue cornmeal
2 cups water
$^1/_2$ teaspoon salt

MAKES 8 TORTILLAS

Put cornmeal in bowl and set aside. Boil water with salt, then slowly pour over cornmeal. Scrape down sides of bowl until combined to make a firm dough. Allow to cool to room temperature. Divide into eight equal-sized balls. Use your hands to press each ball into a very thin round. Bake on preheated griddle, until lightly browned on each side.

THE NEW AMERICANA COOKBOOK

Clover-Leaf Rolls

1 cup skim milk
1 tablespoon sugar
3 tablespoons canola oil
$1/2$ teaspoon salt
1 package dry yeast
2 tablespoons hot water
1 egg
$2^2/_3$ cups all-purpose flour

MAKES 24 ROLLS

Scald milk, then remove from heat. Add sugar, oil and salt.

In a separate bowl, sprinkle yeast over hot (not boiling) water. Wait 5 minutes, then add milk mixture to yeast and beat in egg. Stir in most of the flour, then knead in the rest. Place dough in bowl, cover, and let rise in a warm place until doubled in bulk.

Preheat oven to 400°. Spray muffin tins with non-stick oil. Punch down dough, and roll into 1-inch balls. Squeeze 3 balls together in bottom of each muffin tin. Cover and let rise until double in bulk. Bake about 20 minutes, or until light golden brown on top.

THE NEW AMERICANA COOKBOOK

Quick Carrot-Poppy Seed Bread

1¹/₂ cups grated carrots
³/₄ cup brown sugar
3 tablespoons honey
1 teaspoon lemon juice
1 teaspoon baking soda
3 tablespoons safflower
  oil
3 tablespoons poppy seeds
1 cup boiling water
2 cups all-purpose flour
2 teaspoons baking
  powder
1 teaspoon cinnamon

MAKES ONE 9" x 5" LOAF

Preheat oven to 350°. Spray 9" x 5" bread pan with non-stick vegetable oil.

In a large bowl combine carrots, brown sugar, honey, lemon juice, baking soda, oil, poppy seeds and boiling water. Let rest 10 minutes.

In a separate bowl mix flour, baking powder and cinnamon. Stir in flour mixture just until moistened (do not overmix). Pour into bread pan. Bake 40 minutes or until toothpick inserted in bread comes out clean. Cool in pan 10 minutes before turning bread out onto on wire rack.

Quick breads rise without yeast or the rising and kneading processes associated with yeast breads. A quick bread is usually sweet, often with fruit or nuts. Ingredients are simply stirred together and poured into a pan. Rising agents are often baking powder and eggs. The batter is more moist than a dough, and it quickly goes into and out of the oven!

THE NEW AMERICANA COOKBOOK

Honey Wheat Bread

$^1/_2$ cup 105°-115° water
2 pkgs. active dry yeast
1 egg, beaten
2 tablespoons safflower
   oil
$2^1/_4$ cups lukewarm water
$^1/_2$ teaspoon salt
$^3/_4$ cup honey
4 cups whole-wheat flour
4 cups all-purpose flour

MAKES THREE 5" x 9" LOAVES

Sprinkle yeast over 105°-115° water. Let sit 5 minutes, then stir until yeast is dissolved. Beat in all other ingredients, except flours.

Mix in whole-wheat flour, then all-purpose flour. Knead about 10 minutes, until dough is smooth and satiny. Place in bowl sprayed with non-stick oil, turn to coat all sides. Cover, set in warm place, and let rise until doubled in bulk. Punch dough down, knead again for 5 minutes. Shape into 3 loaves. Place in bread pans sprayed with non-stick oil. Set in warm place to rise until doubled in bulk. Bake 45 minutes in 350° oven.

THE NEW AMERICANA COOKBOOK

Buttermilk Rye Bread

$1/2$ cup very warm water
2 pkgs. active dry yeast
1 cup low-fat buttermilk
$1/2$ cup molasses
3 tablespoons canola oil
1 teaspoon salt
2 tablespoons finely
    grated orange rind
2 tablespoons caraway
    seeds
$2^1/2$ cups finely milled rye
    flour, sifted
3 cups all-purpose flour,
    plus 1 cup flour for
    kneading
1 tablespoon skim milk
2 teaspoons caraway
    seeds

MAKES 2 LOAVES

In a large bowl, dissolve yeast in water. In a small saucepan, warm buttermilk, molasses and oil, then add to yeast mixture. Mix in salt, grated rind and 2 tablespoons caraway seeds. Stir in flours. Turn out and knead 10 minutes on floured board. Spray another bowl with vegetable oil. Place dough in bowl, turning to coat all sides. Cover, and let rise until double in bulk.

Spray two 9" x 5" bread pans with non-stick oil. Punch down dough, and shape into two 9-inch loaves. Place in pans. With a very sharp knife, make four $1/4$-inch deep diagonal slashes in the tops of the loaves. Brush milk over the tops and sprinkle with remaining caraway seeds. Cover, let rise until double in bulk. Bake in 375° oven 35 minutes.

THE NEW AMERICANA COOKBOOK

Potato Bread

$^3/_4$ cup very warm water
1 teaspoon sugar
2 pkgs. active dry yeast
1$^1/_2$ cup mashed potatoes
1$^1/_2$ cups low-fat
    buttermilk
4 tablespoons melted
    butter
$^1/_2$ cup honey
2 teaspoons salt
2 cups oat, rice or whole
    wheat flour
$^1/_2$ cup wheat germ
4$^1/_2$ cups all-purpose flour

MAKES 3 LOAVES

Dissolve the yeast and sugar in water. In a large bowl, mix mashed potatoes, buttermilk, butter, honey and salt. Beat for 2 minutes, then add yeast mixture. Stir in oat, rice or wheat flour, wheat germ and 2 cups all-purpose flour. Turn onto floured board and work in remaining flour. Knead 8 minutes, adding flour as needed to keep dough from sticking. Place in bowl sprayed with non-stick oil, turning dough to coat all sides. Cover, and let rise until double in bulk. Punch down, then shape into 3 loaves. Place each loaf in a 9" x 5" bread pan that's been sprayed with non-stick oil. Let rise until double in bulk. Bake in 375° oven 35 minutes.

Yogurt Corn Bread

1 cup unbleached flour
$^1/_2$ teaspoon baking soda
2 teaspoons double-acting
   baking powder
1 tablespoon brown sugar
1 cup cornmeal
2 cups non-fat plain
   yogurt
2 eggs, beaten
1 tablespoon canola oil

MAKES ONE 9" x 9" PAN

Preheat oven to 350°. Spray a 9" x 9" baking pan with non-stick oil.

Sift together flour, baking soda, baking powder and brown sugar. Stir in cornmeal, yogurt, eggs and oil. Pour into prepared baking pan. Bake about 30 minutes, or until bread is golden brown on top.

Appetizers
and
Finger Food

THE NEW AMERICANA COOKBOOK

CONTENTS

Appetizers can be used as a main dish by doubling the amount of food per serving.

THE NEW AMERICANA COOKBOOK

Crab, Artichoke & Grapefruit Cocktail

3 pink or red grapefruits
12 oz. fresh crabmeat
$\frac{1}{4}$ teaspoon cayenne
2 tablespoons rum
14-oz. can artichoke
    hearts
1 cup low-fat mayonnaise
$\frac{1}{4}$ cup chili sauce
1 tablespoon parsley,
    chopped
1 teaspoon Worcestershire
    sauce
2 tablespoons lemon juice
1 teaspoon black pepper

SERVES 6

Cut grapefruits in half. Remove fruit segments with serrated spoon. Squeeze juice over fruit segments. Clean out grapefruit shells, discarding pith, and set aside. Gently mix grapefruit, crab, cayenne and rum. Drain artichoke hearts, cut in small pieces, press out moisture, and add to mixture.

Cocktail Dressing: Mix remaining ingredients together. Cover and chill.

To Serve: Fill grapefruit shells with crab mixture. Place a heaping spoonful of cocktail dressing on each.

THE NEW AMERICANA COOKBOOK

Tomato, Basil and Sweet Pea Quiche

Pie Shell:
$1^1/_2$ cups cracker crumbs
3 tablespoons canola oil
2 tablespoons skim milk

Filling:
5 stewed tomatoes
1 tablespoon grated onion
1 teaspoon canola oil
$^3/_4$ cup fresh sweet peas
3 eggs, beaten
1 cup skim milk
1 tablespoon fresh basil
1 teaspoon Worcestershire
    sauce
$^3/_4$ cup grated low-fat
    Swiss Lorraine cheese

SERVES 6

Preheat oven to 375°. Spray a 9-inch pie plate with non-stick oil. Put crushed cracker crumbs in a mixing bowl. Sprinkle oil and milk over crumbs. Distribute moisture with a pastry cutter or fork. Press crumbs into pie plate and up the sides. Bake 5 minutes.

Cut tomatoes into bite-sized pieces, drain in sieve for 15 minutes, then gently press out liquid. Sauté onion in oil until nearly clear. Steam peas 5 minutes. Combine all filling ingredients in mixing bowl. Pour into pie shell. Bake 30 minutes or until golden.

THE NEW AMERICANA COOKBOOK

Almond Shrimp Pâté

16 oz. fresh crab meat
2 eggs, separated
$^1/_2$ cup skimmed
    evaporated milk
1 small onion, grated
1 tablespoon soft butter
2 tablespoons brandy
1 tablespoon port wine
1 teaspoon saffron
4 tablespoons almond
    slivers
2 tablespoons flour
$^1/_2$ teaspoon salt
$^1/_2$ teaspoon white pepper

Serve with: crackers

SERVES 6

Preheat oven to 325°, and set kettle of water to boil. Divide crab meat into 3 parts. Put the first part in the blender with egg yolks, process until smooth. Mix the second part with milk. Mix the third part with remaining ingredients (except the egg whites). Whip egg whites until stiff. Lightly combine egg whites with the 3 crab meat mixtures. Spray small ceramic dish with non-stick oil. Pour into dish and cover tightly with aluminum foil. Set pâté dish into larger baking dish. Pour boiling water into larger baking dish, half the height of pâté dish. Bake 1-1$^1/_2$ hours, or until set. Chill, and serve with crackers.

THE NEW AMERICANA COOKBOOK

Roasted Chestnuts

fresh chestnuts

Prick shells of chestnuts with a fork, or they may explode.

Preheat oven to 425°. Roast chestnuts on an oven pan for 15 to 20 minutes.

If you have a fireplace pan or roasting basket, there's nothing more cozy than roasting chestnuts in the fireplace. If you're lacking fireplace cookery, try wrapping chestnuts in triple layers of tin foil.

Chestnuts trees were once very abundant in the northeastern United States, but a severe blight or disease took many of them in the early 1900's. Chestnuts are a versatile food, and much of the world uses them year-round in porridge, pasta flour, candies, and as a grain or side-dish. Chestnuts are both low in fat, and high in protein.

THE NEW AMERICANA COOKBOOK

4th of July Cherry Bombs

1 pint cherry tomatoes
$^1/_2$ cup low-fat cream
    cheese, softened
1 teaspoon finely grated
    onion
1 tablespoon fresh
    chopped cilantro
1 teaspoon cumin
$^1/_2$ teaspoon black pepper
pinch of cayenne
pinch of salt
$^1/_2$ cup small cooked bay
    shrimp
paprika for garnishing

SERVES 6

With a sharp knife, cut tops off cherry tomatoes. Use a small serated grapefruit teaspoon to scoop out pulp. Put pulp in a small mixing bowl with cream cheese. With a fork, mash and blend cream cheese and pulp, and mix in spices.

Drain shrimp and pat dry in paper towels. Chop into small pieces, then gently stir into cream cheese mixture. Place in pastry bag, and squeeze to fill cherry tomatoes. Sprinkle tops with paprika.

Cherry tomato plants are wonderful additions to a sunny patio garden or indoor planter. The variety of cherry tomato plants can be selected to fit the space, lighting and temperature requirements of your location. The vibrant color of these ripening fruits is an added bonus to having your own fresh homegrowns in picking reach all year round.

THE NEW AMERICANA COOKBOOK

Marvelous Mushrooms

SERVES 4

1 lb. fresh mushrooms
(small if possible)
2 cups vegetable bouillon
broth (from cubes)
$1/_4$ cup lemon juice

Tie in a cheesecloth:
12 peppercorns
4" stalk of celery
4 springs parsley
2 cloves garlic
sprig of fresh, or a pinch
of dried, thyme
6 coriander seeds

Wash and trim stem end of mushrooms. If mushrooms are large, cut in quarters, if medium-sized, cut in half.

Combine broth, lemon juice and spice bag in a pot, bring to a boil. Add mushrooms, and stir. Cover pot, reduce heat and simmer 10 minutes. Remove mushrooms with a slotted spoon, and arrange in a serving dish. Rapidly boil down the liquid until it is reduced to about $3/_4$ cup. Remove spice bag. Adjust seasonings to taste. Strain liquid over the mushrooms. Serve hot or cold.

THE NEW AMERICANA COOKBOOK

Black-Eyed Pea Caviar

15-oz. can black-
    eyed peas, drained
15-oz. can white
    hominy, drained
2 medium tomatoes
4 green onions
1 large clove garlic
1 pepper, any color
$1/4$ cup chopped cilantro
2 tablespoons parsley
1 cup picante sauce
    (mild, medium or hot)

Serving Suggestions:
baked tortilla chips
crackers
vegetable dippers

SERVES 6-8

Combine black-eyed peas and hominy in a mixing bowl. Slice tomatoes in half, remove seeds, then chop into small pieces. Using just the white and green tender bases of the green onion, slice into small thin slivers. Crush garlic clove. Dice pepper. Combine all ingredients with black-eyed peas and hominy. Mix well and serve cold.

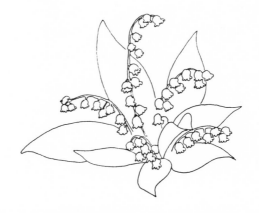

Pesto Guacamole

$^1/_3$ cup non-fat plain
    yogurt
$^1/_3$ cup non-fat cottage
    cheese
2 cloves crushed garlic
$^1/_2$ cup packed fresh basil
    leaves
$^1/_2$ tablespoon olive oil
1 tablespoon grated onion
8 drops hot pepper sauce
1 tablespoon Parmesan
1 tablespoon pine nuts
2 medium sized avocados
2 teaspoons lemon juice
1 cup finely chopped
    tomatoes
salt and pepper to taste

MAKES $1^1/_2$ CUPS

In a blender, whip together yogurt and cottage cheese until smooth. With blender running on high speed, drop in crushed garlic, basil leaves, olive oil, onion, hot pepper sauce, Parmesan cheese and pine nuts. Blend until smooth. In a mixing bowl, mash avacado and sprinkle with lemon juice. Fold blender mixture into avocado, then add chopped tomatoes, salt and pepper.

THE NEW AMERICANA COOKBOOK

Black Bean Dip

You may also find black beans under the name of turtle beans.

2 cups cooked black beans
1 cup non-fat sour cream
3 tablespoons canned
    diced green chiles
1 teaspoon lemon juice
2 tablespoons grated
    onion
$^1/_2$ teaspoon garlic powder
$^1/_2$ teaspoon cumin
$^1/_2$ teaspoon black pepper
$^1/_2$ teaspoon salt

MAKES 3 CUPS

Drain beans and set aside.

Put all other ingredients, except beans, into blender or food processor. When well blended, add 1 cup of beans and process until smooth. Add remaining cup of beans, process on slow speed and stop before beans are completely puréed. The bean texture will add to the quality of this luscious dip.

Naturally low in fat and sodium, high in fiber, protein and complex carbohydrates, the basic bean is an impressive and inexpensive health food. Before cooking, carefully examine for sand or small pebbles, then soak overnight in cold water, removing any that float. The next day, rinse beans twice and simmer in fresh water.

THE NEW AMERICANA COOKBOOK

Rose Salmon Dip

1 lb. fresh salmon fillet
$^1/_3$ cup non-fat cottage
    cheese
3 canned artichoke hearts
1 scallion, chopped
4 drops Tabasco sauce
1 teaspoon Dijon mustard
1 tablespoon lemon juice
1 teaspoon dill
3 tablespoons pimento

MAKES $1^1/_2$ CUPS

Poach salmon fillet in boiling water for 12 minutes. Cut salmon into pieces, and place in blender or food processor with remaining ingredients. Process until smooth. Chill. Serve with French bread, bagels, or crackers.

THE NEW AMERICANA COOKBOOK

Sassy Salsa

My sister Paula created this recipe with some "canning" friends a couple years ago. Her double recipe of 12 pints barely made it to the holidays!

7$\frac{1}{2}$ lbs. tomatoes, peeled,
   cored and chopped
1 lb. yellow onion,
   finely chopped
$\frac{1}{2}$ lb. unpeeled zucchini,
   diced into $\frac{1}{2}$-inch
   cubes
$\frac{1}{2}$ lb. fresh Anaheim
   green chiles, seeded
   and finely chopped
$\frac{1}{4}$ lb. red or green
   Jalepeño chiles,
   seeded and finely
   chopped
1$\frac{1}{2}$ cup cider vinegar
1 teaspoon garlic powder
1 teaspoon salt
kernels from 1 ear corn
2 cups fresh chopped
   cilantro

MAKES 6 PINTS

In a large, non-aluminum pot, combine all ingredients, except fresh cilantro. Cover, and bring to a boil over high heat, stirring frequently. Reduce heat, uncover, and stir occasionally until thickened, about 20-30 minutes. Remove from heat, mix in cilantro.

Sassy Salsa can be canned (see below)or frozen in containers leaving $\frac{1}{2}$-inch headroom for expansion.

To can: Fill sterilized jars with hot salsa, leaving $\frac{1}{2}$-inch headroom. Place jars on rack in boiler half-filled with boiling water, with space between jars. Add boiling water to cover jars 2 inches above their tops. Boil, cover, and process 15 minutes. Use tongs to lift jars, set on towels with several inches between them to cool.

THE NEW AMERICANA COOKBOOK

Bill's Elegant Artichoke Dip

*Serve with French bread or rice crackers
for an exquisite sensory experience.*

14 oz. can artichoke
    hearts in water
4 oz. non-fat cream
    cheese, softened at
    room temperature
$^1/_2$ cup low-fat
    mayonnaise
$^3/_4$ cup grated Parmesan
    cheese

SERVES 4

Preheat oven to 350°. Spray small baking dish with non-stick oil.

Drain artichokes, press out moisture, and chop into small pieces. In a mixing bowl, blend together cream cheese, mayonnaise and Parmesan. Mix in artichoke hearts. Bake 25 minutes in prepared dish. Serve hot.

Salads
and
Fresh Greens

THE NEW AMERICANA COOKBOOK

CONTENTS

THE NEW AMERICANA COOKBOOK

Hot Slaw with Sunflower Seeds

If you've been drying out last season's sunflowers, the seeds should be ready to use in this fresh hot slaw.

$^1/_2$ **cup hulled sunflower seeds**

1 egg

2 tablespoons sugar

2 tablespoons vinegar

$^1/_2$ cup apple cider

1 teaspoon tamari or soy sauce

pinch of pepper

4 cups grated green cabbage

SERVES 4

Lightly toast sunflower seeds on ungreased cookie sheet in 350° oven.

In a large saucepan, whisk together egg, sugar, vinegar, apple cider, tamari or soy sauce and pepper. Stirring constantly, cook over medium-low heat until thickened. Stir in cabbage, cover pan. Cook just until cabbage is hot and beginning to wilt. Place in serving bowl and sprinkle with toasted sunflower seeds. Serve hot.

THE NEW AMERICANA COOKBOOK

Sweet & Sour Kidney Bean Salad

2 cups dried kidney beans
4 tablespoons ketchup
3 tablespoons orange juice
3 tablespoons olive oil
2 tablespoons vinegar
2 teaspoons lemon juice
1 tablespoon dry mustard
3 tablespoons brown
    sugar
1 teaspoon garlic
2 tablespoons finely
    chopped sweet onions
    (Vidalia, red, purple)
1 tablespoon black pepper
2 tablespoons fresh
    parsley

SERVES 9

Soak kidney beans overnight. In the morning, rinse in cold water. Add beans to large pot of boiling water, cover and simmer until tender. Drain and chill.

Combine remaining ingredients together. Mix into chilled beans. Serve cold.

THE NEW AMERICANA COOKBOOK

Pesto Potato Salad
with Cherry Tomatoes

4 cups cooked and diced
    baby red potatoes
$1/4$ cup olive oil
3 tablespoons red wine
    vinegar
1 tablespoon sugar
$1/4$ cup fresh sweet basil,
    finely chopped
1 clove minced garlic
$1/2$ teaspoon black pepper
$1/2$ cup finely chopped
    watercress
2 tablespoons freshly
    chopped parsley
1 pint cherry tomatoes

SERVES 8

Cover and chill diced potatoes in a large bowl. In a separate bowl, combine olive oil, vinegar and spices. When potatoes have thoroughy chilled, pour on dressing and toss. Add whole cherry tomatoes, mix. Chill before serving.

Basil Pesto is an uncooked seasoning made from pounded or blended fresh basil leaves. Traditionally, it also includes pine nuts, garlic, olive oil and Parmesan cheese. Pesto can be used in salad dressings, pasta sauce, sandwich spreads and dips. The fresh flavor released by the ground basil leaves have made Pesto variations quite popular.

THE NEW AMERICANA COOKBOOK

Southwestern Chicken Salad

2 lbs. boneless, skinned
    chicken breasts
2 cups water
2 cups white wine
1 tablespoon lemon juice
3 cloves garlic
2 teaspoons peppercorns
1 teaspoon salt
$1/_2$ cup low-fat mayonnaise
$3/_4$ cup non-fat sour cream
3 tablespoons reserved
    chicken broth
2 hard-boiled eggs, cut into
    small cubes
$1/_4$ cup grated onion,
    Purple or Vadalia
2 tablespoons blue cheese
1 teaspoon lemon juice
$1/_4$ cup chopped cilantro
1 tablespoon ground cumin
1 teaspoon garlic powder
1 teaspoon black pepper

SERVES 6

Place chicken breasts in boiling pot of 2 cups water, wine, lemon juice, garlic cloves, peppercorns and salt. Bring to a boil, skim off scum, and simmer 10 minutes. Cover pot, remove from heat and let chicken rest in hot broth for 40 minutes. Remove chicken, (reserving chicken broth for future use) and cut into $1/_2$-inch cubes. Chill chicken in covered container.

With a wire whisk, combine all remaining ingredients (including 3 tablespoons of the reserved broth). Cover and chill.

When chicken is thoroughly chilled, at least 2 hours, combine with sauce. Garnish plates of Southwestern Chicken Salad with slices of fresh avocado.

THE NEW AMERICANA COOKBOOK

Light Ceasar Salad

Ceasar Dressing:
2 tablespoons low-fat
    mayonnaise
1 raw egg
1 tablespoon olive oil
3 tablespoons lemon juice
3 tablespoons grated
    Parmesan
1 teaspoon anchovy paste
1 teaspoon Worcestershire
    sauce
1 clove garlic, minced
salt and pepper to taste

2 heads romaine lettuce
$1/2$ cup croutons

SERVES 4

In a small bowl, whisk together ingredients for Ceasar Dressing. Cover bowl and chill at least 4 hours.

Wash and tear romaine into pieces. Toss in salad bowl with Ceasar Dressing. Sprinkle croutons on top, serve at once.

THE NEW AMERICANA COOKBOOK

Avocado, Greens and Blood Orange Salad

3 ripe but firm avocadoes
1 large head red leaf
    lettuce
1 bunch watercress,
    shredded
2 large peeled carrots,
    peeled into curls
3 blood oranges

Serve with either:
Zesty Sweet & Sour
    Dressing, page 63
Raspberry-Lime
    Vinaigrette, page 64

SERVES 6

Cut avacodo in half, remove seed. Cut into quarters, then peel. Slice to show shape.

Be sure greens are well washed of grit. Dry in towel and tear into bite-sized pieces. Combine in large bowl with carrot curls. Slice blood oranges in half, remove any seeds, and scoop out sections with serrated teaspoon. Toss blood orange sections into salad. Serve on salad plates with avocado sections arranged on top. Serve with your choice of dressing.

Sprinkling a little lemon juice on a sliced avocado will prevent it from browning. This native American fruit has many vitamins. There are two varieties, a small dark avocado and a large smooth-skinned variety. Both are harvested prior to ripening, but soften quickly once inside. Avocado oil, produced in California, is light and almost flavorless.

THE NEW AMERICANA COOKBOOK

Cucumber and Feta Marinate

2 medium cucumbers
1 Vidalia or sweet onion
10 Greek olives, pitted
$^1/_2$ cup (2 oz.) feta cheese
2 tablespoons olive oil
$^1/_4$ cup white wine vinegar
$^1/_2$ teaspoon garlic powder
$^1/_2$ teaspoon black pepper
pinch of salt

SERVES 4

Peel, halve and slice cucumber into $^1/_4$-inch thick pieces. Halve onion and slice into thin crescents. Slice olives in half lengthwise. Combine cucumber, onion and olives in salad bowl. Crumble feta on top, and toss gently.

Mix remaining ingredients together in a cup, chill for 20 minutes. Pour dressing over cucumber and chill together.

THE NEW AMERICANA COOKBOOK

Crab Louisiana

Sauce: SERVES 4
1/4 cup skim milk
1 tablespoon non-fat   Whisk together skim milk with powdered
   powdered milk   milk. Combine with remaining ingredients of
1 cup non-fat mayonnaise   sauce. Chill.
1/4 cup chili sauce
1 teaspoon Worcestershire   Arrange shredded lettuce in individual serving
   sauce   bowls. Divide crab and place on lettuce.
1/4 cup chopped green   Pour sauce over each portion.
   pepper
1/4 cup chopped green
   onion
2 tablespoons lemon juice
salt and pepper to taste

1 cup shredded lettuce
2 cups cooked crab meat

THE NEW AMERICANA COOKBOOK

Tomato-Olive Aspic

SERVES 6

2 tablespoons gelatin
$^1/_4$ cup cold water
$^1/_2$ cup boiling vegetable
   bouillon broth
2 cups tomato juice
2 tablespoons vinegar
1 tablespoon lemon juice
1 teaspoon paprika
1 teaspoon tarragon
$^1/_2$ teaspoon celery salt
$^1/_2$ teaspoon white pepper
pinch of sugar
$^1/_2$ cup chopped olives
$^1/_2$ cup chopped celery
$^1/_2$ cup minced pimento

Soak gelatin in cold water. Add boiling bouillon broth and stir until gelatin is dissolved. Add tomato juice, vinegar, lemon juice, spices and sugar. Allow to thicken at room temperature.

Pour into mold and chill. When almost ready to set, sprinkle olives, celery and pimento over aspic, and lightly stir. Chill until firm.

To unmold: Briefly set lower part of mold in warm water. Turn out onto platter.

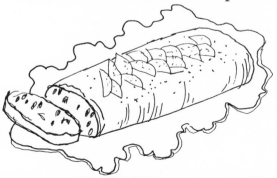

THE NEW AMERICANA COOKBOOK

Peachy-Keen Mint Mold

2 tablespoons gelatin
$^1/_2$ cup cold water
1$^1/_2$ cups peeled and sliced
    peaches
2 cups boiling water
$^1/_4$ cup mint leaves
4 drops green food
    coloring
$^1/_2$ cup sugar
pinch of salt
3 tablespoons lemon juice

SERVES 6

Soak gelatin in cold water.

Briefly poach peaches for 5 minutes in 2 cups boiling water. Remove peaches with a slotted spoon, reserving hot peach juice.

In a separate bowl, pour boiling peach juice over mint leaves. Steep 5-10 minutes, then strain hot liquid into gelatin mixture. Mix in food coloring, sugar, salt and lemon juice.

Rinse, but do not dry inside of mold. Pour gelatin mixture into mold and chill. Just before gelatin sets, arrange peaches in gelatin.

THE NEW AMERICANA COOKBOOK

Zesty Sweet and Sour Dressing

1/3 cup orange juice
1/3 cup tomato purée
6 tablespoons wine vinegar
1 tablespoon sugar
2 tablespoons sesame seeds
3 tablespoons scallion
3 drops Tabasco

MAKES 1 CUP

Combine all ingredients in blender. Process on high until smooth. Adjust seasoning to taste, add salt and pepper if desired. Chill.

Curried Dijon Salad Sauce

2 teaspoons gelatin
2 tablespoons cold water
1 cup vegetable broth
1 teaspoon sugar
1 tablespoon lemon juice
1 tablespoon curry powder
1/4 cup Dijon mustard

MAKES 1 1/3 CUPS

Soak gelatin in cold water. Boil vegetable broth and add to gelatin mixture. Stir in remaining ingredients. Chill. Before serving dressing, beat with a wire whisk.

THE NEW AMERICANA COOKBOOK

Raspberry-Lime Vinaigrette

$^1/_3$ cup raspberries
3 tablespoons lime juice
2 tablespoons sugar
$^1/_4$ cup dry white wine
$^1/_4$ cup red wine vinegar
2 tablespoons parsley
1 clove garlic, minced
salt and pepper to taste

MAKES 1 CUP

Combine all ingredients in glass jar with tight-fitting lid. Shake well. Refrigerator well before serving.

Creamy Peppercorn Dressing

$1/_2$ cup softened non-fat
    cream cheese
1 cup non-fat sour cream
1 tablespoon grated
    Parmesan cheese
1 teaspoon garlic powder
$^1/_2$ teaspoon salt
1 tablespoon fresh
    ground peppercorns

MAKES $1^1/_2$ CUPS

Cut softened cream cheese into small pieces. Combine in blender with sour cream, process until smooth. With blender running, add Parmesan and spices. Chill.

Soups,
Stews
and
Chowders

THE NEW AMERICANA COOKBOOK

CONTENTS

THE NEW AMERICANA COOKBOOK

Crawfish Étouffé

If crawfish are not available, the Étouffé can be made with shrimp.

1 tablespoon safflower oil
1 cup chopped yellow
    onion
1 cup chopped green
    pepper
2 cloves garlic, minced
4 stewed plum tomatoes
1 cup vegetable bouillon
    broth
1 cup tomato juice
1 teaspoon thyme
1 teaspoon saffron
1 bay leaf
$1/2$ teaspoon Tabasco
    sauce
1 cup white rice
2 lbs. cleaned crawfish
3 tablespoons chopped
    parsley
$1/2$ cup skim milk

SERVES 4

In a large skillet, heat oil, sauté onion, pepper and garlic. Add bouillon broth, tomato juice, thyme, saffron, bay leaf and Tabasco sauce. Cover, simmer 10 minutes.

Mix in dry white rice. Chop crawfish into small pieces, and stir in. Simmer 25 minutes. Remove from heat, and add milk. Let set 10 minutes, stir. Serve immediately.

Manhattan Style Clam Chowder

1 cup finely diced onion
³/₄ cup finely diced celery
³/₄ cup diced bell pepper
2 tablespoons canola oil
2 tablespoons flour
3 cups minced clam meat
    cherrystone or quahog
    is preferred
1 cup clam juice
1 cup crushed tomatoes
5 stewed tomatoes,
    finely chopped
1 cup chicken or vegetable
    bouillon broth
2 cups peeled and finely
    diced raw potatoes
1 teaspoon thyme
1 bay leaf
salt and pepper to taste
3 tablespoons fresh
    parsley

SERVES 6

In a large pot, sautée onion, celery and bell pepper in hot canola oil. When onion is nearly clear, stir in flour, then remaining ingredients. Cover and simmer 20 minutes. Uncover and continue cooking until potatoes are tender. Serve with oyster crackers.

NOTE:
About 3 cups minced clam meat is in 1 quart of unshucked clams. If you buy fresh clams, reserve their liquid to use for the clam juice.

THE NEW AMERICANA COOKBOOK

Scalloped Crab Chowder

SERVES 4

2 cups peeled and finely
    diced potatoes
2 cups dry white wine
1 tablespoon grated onion
3 cups skim milk blended
    with 1 cup non-fat
    powdered milk
pinch of thyme
pinch of cayenne
salt and pepper to taste
1 egg yolk, beaten
1 lb. crab meat
$^1/_2$ cup fresh grated
    Parmesan or Gruyère
    cheese

In a covered pot, simmer the potatoes in wine until tender. Drain off half the liquid, leaving potatoes and about 1 cup wine in the pot. Add onion, milk and spices. Warm thoroughly but do not boil. Whisk in egg yolk, cook on medium heat until slightly thickened.

Preheat broiler. Divide crab meat between four oven-proof soup bowls. Ladle soup over crab and sprinkle cheese on soup. Place bowls on cookie sheet, then set under broiler until cheese bubbles. Carefully remove from oven.

THE NEW AMERICANA COOKBOOK

Chicken Mole Soup

SERVES 8

$^1/_2$ cup onion, chopped
    fine
3 cloves garlic, minced
1 tablespoon olive oil
6 canned plum tomatoes
3 lbs. chicken, rinsed and
    cut into small pieces
5 tablespoons canned
    chopped green chiles
7 cups chicken broth
1 cup crushed tomatoes
3 oz. unsweetened baking
    chocolate
1 teaspoon cinnamon
1 teaspoon ground cumin
salt and pepper to taste
$^1/_2$ cup flour

In a large soup pot, sauté onion and garlic in olive oil. Chop plum tomatoes and add to pot with chiles. Stir in chicken, cook until tender. Add 5 cups chicken broth and crushed tomatoes, turn heat to low.

In a separate pot, heat 1 cup of broth, then add chocolate and spices. Stir until chocolate is completely dissolved, then add to soup. In a small dish bake flour in 350° oven for 5 minutes, or until medium brown. In a small pot, whisk remaining cup of broth and browned flour. Cook and stir until thickened, then add to soup. Keep stirring 15 minutes more over medium-high heat until thickened.

Mole comes from the Nahuatl Indian word *molli*, meaning a chile pepper sauce. The chocolate has become an additional favorite, and lends itself well to complement the spicy flavor. A traditional mole is made with turkey, and its meat and broth make an easy substitution to any chicken mole recipe.

THE NEW AMERICANA COOKBOOK

Split Pea and Lentil Stew

This flavor and richness of this stew is brought out by sittingin the refrigerator a day or two, so this recipe makes plenty for now and later!

1 lb. pkg. dried split peas
1 lb pkg. any color lentils
15 cups water
2 cups chopped onion
5 peeled and diced carrots
3 stalks diced celery
3 cloves garlic, minced
3 tablespoons tamari or
    soy sauce
2 teaspoons rosemary
1 small onion stuck with
    8 cloves
3 bay leaves
salt and pepper to taste

Serve with:
croutons

SERVES 6

Rinse split peas and lentils in cold water. Combine all ingredients in a large covered pot. Stirring occasionally, simmer 3-4 hours, adding water if needed. Remove bay leaves and cloved onion. Adjust seasonings to taste.

Serve hot with croutons floating on top.

Salmon Bisque

SERVES 4

$^1/_2$ lb. cooked salmon,
   fresh or canned
$^1/_2$ cup very dry sherry
   (not cooking sherry)
2 teaspoons butter
$^1/_2$ cup very dry red wine
4 tablespoons flour
3 cups skim milk blended
   with 1 cup non-fat
   powdered milk
1 tablespoon
   Worcestershire sauce
salt and pepper to taste

Using a fork, flake salmon into small pieces, while removing bones and skin. Soak flaked salmon in sherry for 1 hour.

Heat butter and red wine, blend in flour to make a roux. Whisk in milk, stirring constantly until thick and smooth. Mix in Worcestershire sauce, salt and pepper. Stir in salmon and heat thoroughly, do not boil.

THE NEW AMERICANA COOKBOOK

Creamy Potato Leek Soup

8 medium-sized potatoes
3 leeks, white stalks only
5 cups water
salt and pepper to taste
skim milk, optional

SERVES 4

Peel and quarter potatoes. Wash leeks thoroughly and cut stalks into 1-inch rounds. Place potatoes, leeks and water in covered pot. Simmer on medium heat until vegetables are very tender, at least 90 minutes. Process potatoes, leeks and their water through food mill (or food processor, but texture will be bland). Stir in salt and pepper. If desired, thin with a little milk. Warm briefly over low heat before serving.

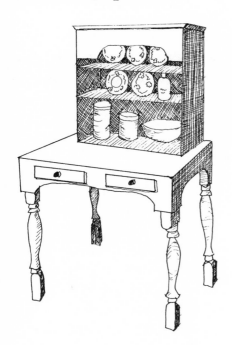

THE NEW AMERICANA COOKBOOK

Apple Squash Soup

3 cups squash purée,
    fresh or canned
1 cup vegetable bouillon
1 cup unsweetened
    applesauce
1 tablespoon flour
1 teaspoon nutmeg
3 tablespoons grated
    onion
$1/2$ cup low-fat buttermilk
salt and pepper to taste

SERVES 6

In a blender, combine squash purée, bouillon broth, applesauce, flour, nutmeg and onion. Blend until smooth. Transfer to covered pot, and simmer 30 minutes.

Remove from heat, stir in buttermilk, salt and pepper. Heat 5 minutes more and serve.

Apple quality is at its peak from July to December. Keep apples stored in a cool, dark and airy place, wrapped in paper with a little space between them. If you find the stock has gone past a tasty eating stage, cooking and baking with these apples is often quite satisfactory. If you get a chance, be sure to try some of the old-fashioned variety apples.

THE NEW AMERICANA COOKBOOK

Rosemary Minestrone

Rosemary Minestrone is outstanding served with Parmesan or pesto.

1 cup small white beans
2 tablespoons olive oil
1 cup thin onion slivers
2 cloves garlic, minced
2 cups vegetable broth
6 cups water
2 cups grated cabbage
2 cups diced potatoes
1 cup chopped celery
2 cups diced zucchini
1 cup cut frozen green
   beans
2 cups chopped stewed
   plum tomatoes
2 tablespoons grated
   lemon rind
1 cup dry spaghetti,
   broken into pieces
2 teaspoons pepper
1 teaspoon salt
2 tablespoons rosemary
$^{1}/_{4}$ cup chopped parsley

SERVES 8

Wash and soak beans overnight in cold water. In the morning, rinse, and drain.

In a large pot, sauté onion and garlic in olive oil until soft, but not brown. Add beans, broth, water, cabbage, potatoes and celery. Bring to a boil, reduce heat and cover pot. Simmer 2 hours. Add remaining ingredients and cook another 30 minutes.

THE NEW AMERICANA COOKBOOK

Northwestern Navy Bean Soup

2 cups dry navy beans
7 cups vegetable
    bouillon broth
1 cup white wine
3 cloves garlic, minced
2 chopped onions
1 cup chopped celery
1 tablespoon lemon juice
2 tablespoons balsamic
    vinegar
2 cups crushed tomatoes
2 cups cooked, chopped
    and drained spinach
2 bay leaves
3 tablespoons parsley
1 teaspoon pepper

SERVES 8

Clean and soak navy beans overnight in cold water. Rinse beans. Combine all ingredients in a large covered pot. Bring to a boil, reduce heat and simmer 3 hours, or until beans are soft and tender. Remove bay leaves.

Serve with garlic bread or low-fat crackers.

THE NEW AMERICANA COOKBOOK

Quick Gazpacho

1 cup peeled, seeded and
    finely diced cucumber
2 cups skinned, seeded
    and finely chopped
    tomatoes
1 cup vegetable broth
1 cup crushed tomatoes
1 tablespoon diced
    pimento
2 teaspoons olive oil
$^1/_2$ red pepper, grated
1 tablespoon fresh dill
pinch of cayenne
1 tablespoon finely
    chopped chives
salt and pepper to taste

SERVES 4

Combine half of the cucumber, tomatoes, vegetable broth, crushed tomatoes and pimento in blender. Process 2 minutes. Add olive oil and blend another minute.

Pour into a bowl and stir in remaining cucumber, tomatoes, broth, pimento and other ingredients. Chill well before serving.

THE NEW AMERICANA COOKBOOK

Baked Onion Soup

1 1/2 lbs. peeled onions
1 tablespoon safflower oil
1 tablespoon sugar
1 teaspoon black pepper
1 tablespoon paprika
2 bay leaves
1 teaspoon tamari or soy sauce
5 tablespoons flour
6 cups vegetable bouillon broth
1/2 cup grated Gruyère cheese

Serve with toasted French or crusty light bread

SERVES 4

Cut onions in half, then slice with the grain into 1/8-inch slivers. Over medium heat, heat oil in a soup pot, then add onions. Cover pot and allow onions to wilt for 20 minutes. Sprinkle sugar over onions, toss and cook, uncovered, 10 minutes. Add pepper, paprika, bay leaves, and tamari or soy sauce. Stir in flour, one tablespoon at a time. With a wire whisk, mix in bouillon broth, two cups at a time. Simmer, uncovered, 10 minutes.

Preheat oven to 300°. Ladle soup into oven proof bowls, and set bowls on baking sheet. Bake 25 minutes then sprinkle 2 tablespoons grated cheese on each bowl. Bake 5 minutes more.

Main Meal Dishes

THE NEW AMERICANA COOKBOOK

CONTENTS

* Suitable for outdoor cooking or grilling

Any fish, cooked by any means, generally requires only 10 minutes of cooking time for each inch of thickness, measured at its thickest part.

THE NEW AMERICANA COOKBOOK

Mom's Chicken Supreme

This is one of my mother's best recipes,
and that's saying a lot!

2 chicken bouillon cubes
2 tablespoons lemon juice
$^1/_4$ cup white wine
1 teaspoon white pepper
1 teaspoon garlic powder
2 tablespoons canola oil
3 tablespoons flour
4 large boneless, skinned
    chicken breasts
1 tablespoon canola oil
$^1/_2$ teaspoon salt
$^1/_2$ teaspoon black pepper
1 cup fine bread crumbs
1 medium head broccoli
2 - 14 oz. cans artichoke
    hearts, sliced
8 medium mushrooms,
    sliced to show shape
4 slices provolone cheese

SERVES 4

Boil 2 cups water, add bouillon cubes and stir until dissolved. Mix in lemon juice, wine, white pepper and garlic. Bring to a simmer.

In a separate pan, heat 2 tablespoons oil, then blend in flour. Whisk into simmering broth and cook 10 minutes while stirring constantly. Remove from heat.

Rub chicken breasts with 1 tablespoon oil. Sprinkle with salt and black pepper. Dip breasts in bread crumbs until coated. Bake in 375° oven 40 minutes, or until chicken meat is white inside. Cover with a slice of cheese.

While chicken is baking, prepare sauce. Cut broccoli florets into $^1/_2$-inch pieces. Add florets, artichokes and mushrooms to sauce, and return to heat. Simmer vegetables in sauce for 5-7 minutes. Serve hot with sauce spooned over baked breasts.

THE NEW AMERICANA COOKBOOK

Brandied Shrimp Scampi

2 teaspoons butter
2 teaspoons olive oil
3 cloves pressed garlic
4 scallions, white stalks
　　only, chopped fine
1$\frac{1}{2}$ lbs. shrimp, peeled
　　and deveined
2 teaspoons lemon juice
3 tablespoons brandy
salt and pepper to taste

Optional:
oven-toasted sesame seeds

SERVES 4

Spray a large skillet with non-stick oil. Heat butter and olive oil in skillet, then add pressed garlic and chopped scallions.

Pat dry shrimp in a towel. Raise heat under pan, toss in shrimp and sear. Shake and toss shrimp in pan to brown on all sides.

Before removing from heat, sprinkle shrimp with lemon juice and brandy. The liquid should evaporate, but the flavors will remain. Toss with salt and pepper. If desired, sprinkle with toasted sesame seeds.

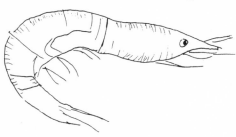

THE NEW AMERICANA COOKBOOK

Oven-Fried Chicken

4 egg whites
3 lbs. boneless, skinned
    chicken breasts
1 cup fine bread crumbs
1 cup cornmeal
2 tablespoons paprika
2 teaspoons garlic powder
1 teaspoon salt
1 teaspoon pepper

SERVES 6

Preheat oven to 375°. Spray non-stick baking sheet with 3 coats non-stick oil.

Whisk egg whites until foamy. Rinse chicken breasts, pat dry, and leave wrapped in towel. In a separate bowl, combine bread crumbs, cornmeal and spices.

Dip chicken breasts in egg whites, coat in spiced crumbs and cornmeal, then place on baking sheet. Bake 20 minutes, flip breasts, and bake 15 minutes more or until meat is white inside.

THE NEW AMERICANA COOKBOOK

Maryland Crab Cakes with Green Sauce

$1^1/_2$ lbs. cleaned crab meat
$^1/_2$ cup diced red pepper
1 tablespoon white wine
$^1/_3$ cup non-fat
    mayonnaise
1 teaspoon Dijon mustard
2 teaspoons
    Worcestershire sauce
1 egg, beaten
$^1/_4$ cup bread crumbs
salt and pepper to taste
2 tablespoons canola oil

Green Sauce:
$^3/_4$ cup canned green chili
    peppers, drained and
    chopped
3 tablespoons vinegar
2 teaspoons sugar

SERVES 4

Clean crab meat. Pat dry in a paper towel.

Simmer red pepper in wine. In a mixing bowl, combine pepper with remaining ingredients, except canola oil. Let set 15 minutes, then form into 3-inch cakes. Spray large skillet with non-stick oil. Coat with oil. Fry crab cakes on each side until browned.

Green Sauce: In a small saucepan, simmer all ingredients 20 minutes. Serve in a small demi-cup on the side of crab cakes.

THE NEW AMERICANA COOKBOOK

Grilled Swordfish Kabobs

Most grilled items will retain their tender texture
if first soaked in a flavorful marinate.

2 lbs. swordfish, cut into
    1-inch cubes
$^1/_2$ cup white wine
$^1/_2$ cup lemon juice
1 teaspoon garlic powder
1 teaspoon pepper
1 tablespoon tamari or
    soy sauce

Optional:
cherry tomatoes and/or
cucumber cubes

SERVES 6

Place swordfish cubes (and cherry tomatoes and/or cucumber cubes) in shallow pan.

Combine remaining marinade ingredients together. Pour over fish (and vegetables) and marinate at least 30 minutes, stirring occasionally to coat.

Preheat broiler, or prepare grill. Thread fish (alternately with vegetables) on skewers. Broil or grill about 10 minutes, turning and basting frequently.

Create your own Marinate: Most white fish, swordfish, tuna, and ground fish will be amply seasoned after an hour or two in a marinate. Try experimenting with liquid bases such as red or white wine, balsamic vinegar, olive oil, tamari, clam juice, chicken stock, lemon juice and vermouth. Add your favorite spices, cover, and chill while marinating.

THE NEW AMERICANA COOKBOOK

Scallops and Mushrooms Au Gratin

1$^{1}/_{2}$ lbs. scallops, whole if
    small, quartered or
    halved if large
1$^{1}/_{2}$ cups dry vermouth
1 bay leaf
2 cups sliced mushrooms
1 tablespoon butter
2 tablespoons white wine
3 tablespoons flour
1 cup skim milk blended
    with $^{1}/_{4}$ cup non-fat
    powdered milk
$^{1}/_{2}$ teaspoon salt
$^{1}/_{2}$ teaspoon white pepper
1 teaspoon freshly
    squeezed lemon juice
$^{2}/_{3}$ cup grated low-fat
    Swiss Lorraine cheese

SERVES 4

Boil vermouth with bay leaf. Poach scallops and mushrooms in the boiling liquid for 2 minutes, then remove from heat, cover pot and let set 10 minutes. With a slotted spoon, transfer scallops and mushrooms to a bowl. Remove bay leaf, boil down poaching liquid to about 1$^{1}/_{2}$ cups.

In a saucepan, heat butter and white wine. Blend in flour, cook 1 minute. Remove from heat and whisk in milk, poaching liquid, salt and pepper. Simmer and stir over medium heat. If too thick, add a little milk.

Remove sauce from heat, stir in lemon juice. Fold into scallops and mushrooms, transfer to baking dish. Sprinkle with grated cheese. Just before serving, place casserole 5-inches under broiler until bubbly and light brown.

THE NEW AMERICANA COOKBOOK

Chicken Americana

6 large skinned chicken breasts
2 tablespoons olive oil
2 cups all-purpose flour
8 fresh plum tomatoes
1 cup sliced mushrooms
12 pitted olives, halved
1 tablespoon capers
2 cloves minced garlic
1 teaspoon rosemary
1 teaspoon basil
1 teaspoon pepper
1 medium onion
2 red peppers
2 green peppers
1/3 cup white wine

SERVES 6

Pat chicken dry then rub with olive oil. Put flour small bag, and place breasts one at a time in bag, shake to coat. Spray 2-inch deep baking dish with non-stick oil. Bake coated breasts in dish at 400° for 20 minutes.

Dice tomatoes into small cubes, slice onions into slivers, and cut peppers into rings. Combine these vegetables with remaining ingredients in large saucepan. Simmer for 30 minutes. Leaving chicken breasts in pan, evenly spread sauce over them. Cover pan with tin foil and bake 25 minutes at 400°, then remove foil and bake 15 minutes more.

THE NEW AMERICANA COOKBOOK

Lemon Trout

4 fillets of trout, sized to
  suit appetites
1 medium onion, thinly
  sliced in rounds
salt and pepper to taste
12 round lemon slices
  with seeds removed

SERVES 4

Preheat oven to 400° or prepare outdoor grill and allow fire to burn down to hot coals.

Make a "packet" for each serving of trout: fold a double thickness of tin-foil into a 12-inch square. Place trout in middle of foil and sprinkle with salt and pepper. Place 3 lemon slices on each trout and cover with onion rounds. Fold in ends of foil and crease. Bring sides of foil together over fish, fold edges together, and crease into a $\frac{1}{2}$-inch seam. Continue folding and creasing until flat against fish. Place fish packet in oven or on grill. Cook packet 4 minutes on each side.

Brook trout is the best of the trouts, and they are commonly stocked throughout North American rivers and steams. Brook trout have a delicate flavor and can be substituted in most recipes for salmon, catfish or rainbow trout. These fish are best eaten as fresh as you can get them, right out of the river and into the frying pan!

THE NEW AMERICANA COOKBOOK

Maple-Mustard Salmon

1 $^{1}/_{2}$ lbs. fresh salmon
    fillets
2 tablespoons Dijon
    mustard
$^{1}/_{4}$ cup maple syrup
1 teaspoon lemon juice
1 teaspoon white pepper
pinch of salt
1 teaspoon melted butter

SERVES 4

Preheat broiler. Check salmon fillets for bones and remove with pliers. Blend mustard, maple syrup, lemon juice, pepper and salt.

Spray broiler pan with non-stick oil. Place fillets on pan and brush with butter. Coat with maple-mustard sauce. Place under broiler, leaving oven door tipped open. Salmon is done when inner flesh is light pink. Serve with juices from pan spooned over fish.

Sauce can also be used to baste salmon on outside grill.

THE NEW AMERICANA COOKBOOK

White Fish
with Piquant Tomato Sauce

2$^{1}/_{2}$ lbs. white fish
    fillets
1$^{1}/_{2}$ cups white wine
1 cup chopped yellow
    onion
1 tablespoon olive oil
1 tablespoon lemon juice
1 teaspoon oregano
2 tablespoons tiny capers
3 cups canned Italian
    plum tomatoes,
    finely chopped,
    with their juices
1 tablespoon butter

SERVES 6

Preheat oven to 350°. Place fillets in an oven dish and pour wine over fish. Poach in oven just until cooked through. Drain liquid and set aside. Cover fish to keep warm.

In a saucepan, sauté onion in olive oil. When onion is clear, add lemon juice, oregano, capers, and tomatoes with juice. Rapidly boil down until sauce is very thick. Reduce heat.

Add poaching liquid to tomato sauce. Rapidly boil down until about 3 cups remain. Stir in butter. Serve immediately with Piquant Tomato Sauce spooned over fish.

THE NEW AMERICANA COOKBOOK

Almond Baked Catfish

1¹/₂ lbs. lean catfish fillets
1 lime, juiced
2 egg whites
¹/₂ cup almond slivers
1 cup cornmeal
1 teaspoon thyme
1 teaspoon black pepper
¹/₂ teaspoon cayenne
1 teaspoon ground
    coriander

SERVES 6

Preheat oven to 375°. Spray baking pan with non-stick oil. Trim any excess fat from catfish, and brush with lime juice.

Whisk egg whites in a medium bowl. Process almond slivers with cornmeal in blender until finely ground. Transfer almond-cornmeal mixture to a wide bowl, add spices.

Dip catfish in eggs, then coat in almond-cornmeal. Place in prepared baking pan and let rest 15 minutes. Bake 15 minutes, or until crust is lightly browned.

THE NEW AMERICANA COOKBOOK

Chicken Pot Pie

Crust:
2 cups unbleached flour
$\frac{1}{4}$ cup canola oil
6 tablespoons cold skim
    milk

Filling:
1 cup pearl onions, cut
    in halves
$\frac{1}{2}$ cup diced celery
2 tablespoon white wine
1 cup pre-cooked peas
1 cup finely diced carrots
2 cups finely diced cooked
    chicken meat
1 teaspoon minced garlic
1 teaspoon rosemary
salt and pepper to taste
$\frac{1}{2}$ cup skim milk
1 cup chicken broth
2 egg yolks, beaten

SERVES 4

Put flour in bowl, make well in center and add liquids. Use pastry cutter or knives to cut liquids into flour until mixture resembles texture of peas. Divide and press into eight balls, then chill 15 minutes in refrigerator. Roll out dough to make top and bottom crusts for four pot pies. Line pie plates with bottoms. After filling, place top crust on pie, and press edges together while fluting with fork. Trim excess dough.

Simmer onion, celery and white wine in saucepan. When celery is tender, add remaining ingredients, except egg yolks. Heat well. Whisk in egg yolks and cook until thickened. Lightly spray inside of pot pie crust with non-stick oil before filling with chicken filling. Bake in 375° oven 35 minutes or until top is golden brown.

THE NEW AMERICANA COOKBOOK

The Lobster Bake by Sunset

6 cups sea water
seaweed rinsed of sand,
    or leaves of 1 head
    iceberg lettuce
6 dozen steamer clams
6 lobsters, 1-1¹/₂ lbs. each
6 ears of corn, husked
6 potatoes wrapped in
    double layers of tin-
    foil

Serve seafood with:
bowls of lemon juice and
    clam juice mixed with
    salt and pepper to
    taste

Bring along:
corn and potato fixings
lobster crackers and picks

SERVES 6

This meal can also be prepared on a stove top.

Preparation: Scrub clams, discarding any with broken shells or that do not close tightly when handled. Tie clams by the dozen, in squares of cheesecloth tied with string. Allow room in bags for clams to open.

Dig a 3 foot deep hole in the sand or gravel. Build a fire of driftwood. Let it die down and turn to hot coals about 2 hours before sunset. Set 24-quart steamer pot in hole over embers. Pour sea water into pot and place 2 inches of seaweed or lettuce leaves in water.

Place lobsters and corn in pot. Cover with 4-inches rinsed seaweed or lettuce. Put clam bags on seaweed and cover pot. Place wrapped baking potatoes around base of pot. Fill in hole with sand or gravel, covering potatoes and pot. Leave covered about 1¹/₂ hours. Carefully dig up lobster pot and potatoes.

THE NEW AMERICANA COOKBOOK

Kickin' Chicken Barbecue

This barbecue can be made as hot as you'd like by varying the amount of cayenne pepper, or try a little hot pepper sauce instead.

1 medium onion
2 teaspoons canola oil
$1^1/_2$ cups catsup
1 cup red wine
$^1/_2$ cup cider vinegar
$^1/_4$ cup brown sugar
2 teaspoons lemon juice
2 tablespoons
    Worcestershire sauce
$^1/_2$ teaspoon liquid smoke
$^1/_8$ teaspoon cayenne,
    and maybe more
1 teaspoon ginger
1 tablespoon garlic powder
1 bay leaf
$^1/_2$ teaspoon black pepper
2 tablespoons flour

Lean skinned chicken

MAKES 3 CUPS SAUCE

Dice onion into small pieces. In a large saucepan, sautée onion in oil. Whisk in remaining ingredients, and simmer 30 minutes or until thickened. Remove bay leaf.

Grill chicken on barbecue. When almost cooked through, baste with a thick coat of sauce, flip and baste second side. Continue basting and flipping to cover in three coats of barbecue, being careful that sauce does not burn. Serve with extra sauce on the side.

Pasta, Beans, and Grains

THE NEW AMERICANA COOKBOOK

CONTENTS

Chicken Noodle Casserole

1 tablespoon canola oil
2 shallots, chopped
2 minced garlic cloves
$^1/_2$ cup diced celery
3 tablespoons flour
$3^1/_2$ cups chicken stock
$^1/_2$ cup white wine
2 egg yolks, beaten
4 cups cooked chicken,
   cut into $^1/_2$-inch cubes
$^1/_4$ cup chopped parsley
   leaves

1 lb. pkg. dried thin egg
   noodles, boiled and
   drained

SERVES 6

Preheat oven to 350°. Spray a large casserole with non-stick oil.

In a large pan, heat oil. Sauté shallots, garlic and celery. Put flour in a small baking pan and place in oven 5 minutes, until light brown. Blend baked flour into vegetable sauté. Slowly whisk in chicken stock, white wine and beaten egg yolks. When sauce is thickened, stir in chicken and parsley. Heat 5 minutes.

Gently fold cooked noodles into chicken and sauce. Transfer to prepared casserole, cover. Bake 15 minutes, then remove cover and bake 10 minutes more.

THE NEW AMERICANA COOKBOOK

Lasagne with Roasted Bell Peppers

1 lb. red bell peppers
1 lb. green bell peppers
2 teaspoons olive oil
1 onion, chopped
2 cloves minced garlic
16 oz. can Italian-style
    plum tomatoes
$\frac{1}{2}$ cup dry white wine
2 tablespoons tomato
    paste
1 teaspoon each rosemary,
    pepper, basil, oregano
6 ruffled lasagne noodles

Bechamel Sauce:
3 tablespoons flour
$1\frac{1}{4}$ cups skim milk
1 garlic clove, minced
a pinch each of: salt,
    nutmeg, and pepper
$\frac{1}{2}$ cup fresh grated
    Parmesan cheese

SERVES 4

Char peppers in broiler, turning frequently. Place in paper bag 10 minutes, then peel off skins. Seed peppers and cut into 2" strips.

In a large saucepan, sauté onion and garlic in oil. Chop plum tomatoes and add to saucepan with their juice, wine, tomato paste and spices. Simmer until liquid is reduced by half.

Boil noodles until tender but firm to the bite. Drain, spread on towels and pat dry. Cut into 8-inch lengths, reserving ends.

Sauce: In a saucepan, blend flour and $\frac{1}{4}$ cup milk. Whisk in remaining milk and spices. Stirring constantly, simmer for 2 minutes. Remove from heat, stir in Parmesan cheese.

Spray 8" x 8" pan with non-stick oil. Make 3 layers as follows: tomato sauce, 2 noodles and ends, bechamel sauce, and peppers. Dot top with bechamel. Bake at 400° for 30 minutes.

THE NEW AMERICANA COOKBOOK

Chili by Wild Willie

2 cups dried pinto beans
2 tablespoons olive oil
2 cups chopped onion
3 cloves crushed garlic
2 fresh jalapeño peppers
6 cups vegetable broth
2 cups crushed tomatoes
$^1/_4$ cup balsamic vinegar
5 stewed plum tomatoes,
    chopped, and juices
1 cup diced green pepper
1 cup diced red pepper
1 cup corn kernels
1 cup diced zucchini
$^1/_2$ teaspoon cayenne
1 tablespoon cumin
1 tablespoon oregano
$^1/_2$ cup chopped cilantro
    (fresh coriander)
2 teaspoons brown sugar
1 tablespoon paprika
salt and pepper to taste

SERVES 8

Soak beans overnight in cold water. Drain, and boil in 6 cups fresh water until tender, about 3-4 hours. Drain.

Core, seed, scrape inner membrane and chop jalapeños, being careful not to touch face, eyes or children before washing your hands from the hot pepper oil. In a large pot, heat oil. Add onion, garlic and jalapeños. Cook until onions are clear and jalapeños are wilted.

Add cooked pinto beans and all other ingredients to the pot. Leave uncovered, bring to a boil, then reduce heat and simmer 45 minutes. Adjust spices to taste. (If chili is too spicy, it can be served over a bed of rice.)

Other go-along favorites are non-fat sour cream, corn bread, grated Monterey Jack or low-fat Cheddar, and soft tortillas.

THE NEW AMERICANA COOKBOOK

Shells Stuffed with Crab Ricotta

¹/₂ lb. large pasta shells
    for stuffing
2 teaspoons safflower oil
2 cups part-skim Ricotta
    cheese
¹/₂ cup grated low-fat
    Swiss Lorraine cheese
1 lb. fresh or canned crab
    meat
2 teaspoons garlic powder
1 teaspoon white pepper
2 tablespoons parsley
¹/₂ cup chopped onion
¹/₂ cup chopped pepper
1 clove garlic, minced
2 teaspoons olive oil
2 cups chopped plum
    tomatoes and juice
¹/₄ cup tomato paste
1 bay leaf
1 teaspoon oregano
salt and pepper to taste

SERVES 6

Rapidly boil pasta shells in a large quantity of water until tender, but firm to the bite. Drain, return to pot and toss with safflower oil to keep them from sticking together.

In a mixing bowl, combine Ricotta, Swiss Lorraine, crab meat, garlic powder, white pepper and parsley. Stuff filling into shells and place in a large baking pan that's been sprayed with non-stick oil.

Sauté onion, pepper and garlic in olive oil. Add remaining ingredients and rapidly cook down until sauce has thickened. Remove bay leaf and spoon over stuffed shells. Bake in 350° oven for 30 minutes.

THE NEW AMERICANA COOKBOOK

Backwater Wild Rice Ring

1 cup wild rice
4 cups water
1 teaspoon salt
1 tablespoon canola oil
$^1/_2$ cup chopped onion
1 clove garlic, minced
$^1/_2$ cup finely chopped
   celery
$^1/_2$ cup chopped
   mushrooms
$^1/_4$ cup dry sherry
1 teaspoon nutmeg
1 small can water
   chestnuts
1 cup non-fat sour cream
1 tablespoon chopped
   parsley

SERVES 6

Wash wild rice several times, pouring off particles that float. Boil water and salt, then stir in rice. Cover and simmer 40 minutes or until tender. Do not stir while cooking.

Sauté onion, garlic, celery and mushrooms in oil. Turn off heat, add sherry and nutmeg. Combine with cooked rice. Press into 7-inch ring mold that has been sprayed with non-stick oil. Place ring mold in a pan of hot water in the oven. Bake at 350° for 20 minutes. Loosen edges and turn onto serving platter. Drain water chestnuts, toss with sour cream and parsley, salt and pepper to taste, and fill center of ring. Serve at once.

Wild rice grows along the waterways of the northern United States. In the Minnesota Backwaters, wild rice is harvested by bending the tall grasses into a canoe and beating the seeds off the stems. The grains are prized for their rich flavor, and the handwork involved in harvesting. High in protein, their nutritional content is actually similar to wheat.

Shrimp Creole

2 tablespoons canola oil
4 tablespoons flour
1½ cups vegetable
    bouillon broth
1 tablespoon canola oil
2 tablespoons dry sherry
¾ cup chopped onion
¾ cup chopped green
    pepper
2 cups chopped stewed
    tomatoes and juice
1 bay leaf
1 teaspoon brown sugar
½ teaspoon cayenne
salt and pepper to taste
1½ lbs. pre-cooked and
    deveined shrimp,
    thawed and drained
4 cups cooked rice

SERVES 4

Heat 2 tablespoons oil in a large saucepan over low heat. Make a roux by blending in flour and brown. Whisk in vegetable broth, and cook over medium-low heat.

In a separate saucepan, sauté onion and green pepper in 1 tablespoon oil and sherry until browned. Stir in stewed tomatoes and their juice, bay leaf, brown sugar, cayenne, salt and pepper. Rapidly cook down over medium-high heat until liquid is reduced by half. Stir into flour roux, cook until thickened. Add shrimp and simmer for 5 minutes.

Serve over bed of hot rice.

Cheddar Risotto

3 shallots, diced
2 tablespoons olive oil
$1/2$ cup grated carrot
1 clove garlic, minced
2 cups dry arborio rice
$1/2$ cup Marsala
1 tablespoon powdered
    vegetable stock or
    crushed bouillon cube
1 cup frozen peas, thawed
$1/2$ cup red pepper, diced
2 canned tomatoes,
    chopped and drained
1 tablespoon butter
1 teaspoon black pepper
$1/2$ cup fresh grated
    Cheddar cheese

SERVES 4 (8 AS A SIDE DISH)

In a large saucepan, sauté shallots in oil. Add carrot and garlic, cook until shallots are clear. Stir in rice, then turn heat to high and add Marsala. Cook until liquid is reduced by half. Reduce heat to medium.

In a separate pot, mix powdered stock or bouillon into 6 cups boiling water. Add hot broth to risotto, $1/2$ cup at a time. Stir, and allow rice to absorb liquid after each addition. Some liquid will remain after final addition of broth. Add peas, pepper and tomato, cook 5 minutes. Add more boiling liquid if needed to make rice creamy and soft. Just before serving stir in butter, pepper and Cheddar.

Cheese has been called "milk's leap to immortality." A good sharp Cheddar cheese is aged about 3 years, while undergoing an elaborate cutting and layering process. In the cooler North American climates, hard cheeses can ripen slowly and develop their full flavor. Knowledgeable cheese makers can keep Cheddars cellared for years.

THE NEW AMERICANA COOKBOOK

Pine Nut Bread Stuffing

1 tablespoon canola oil
1 cup chopped onion
$^1/_2$ cup chopped celery
2 tablespoons pine nuts
1 teaspoon saffron
1 teaspoon sage
2 tablespoons parsley
salt and pepper to taste
2 cups plain, unsalted
    croutons
1 cup warm skim milk

SERVES 4

Sauté onion, celery and pine nuts in oil. Stir in spices, then croutons. Heat well. Slowly pour in warm milk. Serve immediately as a side-dish, or use for stuffing.

THE NEW AMERICANA COOKBOOK

Maple Sugar Baked Beans

1 lb. pinto beans
1 teaspoon olive oil
2 cups chopped onion
1 clove minced garlic
2 tablespoons fresh
    grated ginger
2 cups apple cider
2 cups water
1 cup maple syrup
$\frac{1}{4}$ cup brown sugar
1 tablespoon dry mustard
2 bay leaves
pinch of allspice
pinch of cloves
salt and pepper to taste

SERVES 10

Clean twigs and stones from beans, wash and soak overnight in cold water. The next morning, drain beans and rinse.

Heat olive oil in saucepan. Sauté onion, garlic and ginger until lightly browned. Combine beans, onion sauté, and remaining ingredients. Spray a large casserole or bean pot with non-stick oil, transfer mixture into prepared baking dish, and cover.

Bake in 350° oven 3 hours, or until tender, adding water as needed. Just before beans are finished, remove lid and brown.

THE NEW AMERICANA COOKBOOK

Lima Beans with Sautéed Garlic

1 lb. dried baby lima
   beans
2 tablespoons safflower
   oil
2 shallots
6-8 cloves garlic, minced
3 tablespoons vermouth
1 teaspoon ground cloves
1 teaspoon black pepper
1 teaspoon savory
1 teaspoon sage
2 tablespoons fresh
   parsley

SERVES 6

Wash lima beans and soak overnight. In the morning, drain, and put beans in a large pot of boiling water. Cover and simmer until tender, about 1 hour. Do not allow beans to overcook and become mushy.

Just before beans are finished cooking, heat oil in saucepan. Slice shallots into crescent-shaped pieces. Sauté shallots and garlic in oil. Mix in vermouth and spices, reduce heat.

Drain lima beans, and stir into saucepan with garlic sauce. Serve at once.

The use of garlic in America came from the recipes of the European immigrants. Although long prevalent in American homes with strong cultural traditions, garlic was not popular until the 1960's, when diverse ethnic cooking styles became fashionable. Today, garlic is commonly used in many American recipes.

Vegetables
and
Sauces

THE NEW AMERICANA COOKBOOK

CONTENTS

THE NEW AMERICANA COOKBOOK

Carrot-Beet Julienne

$^1/_2$ cup water
2 cups carrots, peeled
    and cut diagonally
    into thin strips
2 cups beets, peeled and
    cut diagonally into
    thin strips
1 teaspoon butter
1 tablespoon honey
2 tablespoons orange juice
1 teaspoon vinegar
pinch of salt
1 teaspoon lemon juice
$^1/_2$ teaspoon chopped
    parsley

SERVES 4

In a saucepan, boil water over medium-high heat. Add all ingredients, except parsley. Continue to cook until water evaporates, about 10 minutes.

Remove from heat, stir to coat vegetables. Sprinkle with parsley before serving.

THE NEW AMERICANA COOKBOOK

Fried Green Tomatoes

Keep the oil very hot and very little oil will be absorbed by the tomatoes. These are a favorite treat and one more great reason to grow your own!

$^3/_4$ cup all-purpose flour
pinch of salt
1 teaspoon black pepper
1 teaspoon basil
6 large green tomatoes
olive oil for frying
8 lemon wedges

SERVES 8

In a small mixing bowl, combine flour, salt, pepper and basil. Cut a thin layer of skin off top and bottom of tomatoes, and discard. Slice tomatoes into $^1/_4$-inch thick rounds.

Spray a large frying pan with non-stick oil. Pour 1 tablespoon olive oil into pan and preheat over medium-high. Dip each tomato into the flour to coat top and bottom sides. Fry until golden brown, about 5 minutes on each side. Drain on paper towels. Use about 1 tablespoon olive oil for each batch of fried tomatoes. Garnish with lemon wedges.

THE NEW AMERICANA COOKBOOK

Tomato Corn Succotash

4 whole peeled tomatoes
    (fresh or canned)
salt and pepper to taste
2 cups corn kernels
    (preferably cut from
    fresh cooked corn)
4 tablespoons brown
    sugar
2 tablespoons bread
    crumbs

SERVES 4

Preheat oven to 350°. Spray a small casserole with non-stick oil.

Chop peeled tomatoes, mix with salt and pepper. Spread half of the corn in prepared casserole, then cover with half the tomatoes. Sprinkle 2 tablespoons brown sugar on top. Repeat process for second layers of corn, tomatoes and brown sugar. Cover with bread crumbs. Bake 20 minutes, serve hot.

Succotash is the Indian name for corn cooked into a porridge, or baked together with beans or vegetables. The early colonists made many improvisations on succotash, including the addition of salt. Sometimes the corn kernels were "thribbled," which meant the grains were cooked until they had swelled to three times their original size.

THE NEW AMERICANA COOKBOOK

Green Beans Amandine

1 lb. frozen green beans
1 teaspoon butter
2 tablespoons white wine
3 tablespoons sliced
    almonds
pinch of salt
$^{1}/_{2}$ teaspoon pepper

SERVES 4

Warm green beans in covered pot until tender, but not limp. Drain and return to pot. While green beans are cooking, toast sliced almonds on baking sheet in 300° oven, then sauté in butter and wine. Pour over drained green beans. Add salt and pepper, toss.

Hot Stuffed Chiles

4 chiles: poblana (ancho),
    Mexi-bell or Anaheim
1 cup corn kernels
$^{1}/_{4}$ cup chopped sweet onion
$^{1}/_{3}$ cup chopped bell pepper
2 tablespoons fresh cilantro
1 cup grated low-fat
    Cheddar cheese
$^{1}/_{4}$ cup bread crumbs

SERVES 4

Cut chiles in half lengthwise, remove seeds and membranes. Spray baking pan with non-stick oil, and place chile halves on pan. Combine remaining ingredients to make stuffing, and fill chiles. Bake at 350° for 45 minutes. Serve with non-fat sour cream or yogurt to mellow. These chiles are hot!

THE NEW AMERICANA COOKBOOK

Honey-Glazed Turnips

8 small whole turnips
1 teaspoon butter
1 tablespoon safflower oil
2 tablespoons honey
2 teaspoons lemon juice
salt and pepper to taste

SERVES 4

Peel turnips and cut into quarters. Simmer in boiling water about 30 minutes. Combine remaining ingredients in a small saucepan and warm over low heat. When turnips are tender place in serving bowl and coat with sauce.

Roasted Garlic

SERVES 6

6 whole heads garlic
³/₄ cup vegetable bouillon broth

Preheat oven to 350°. Remove outer papery peel from garlic heads, but leave heads intact. Place garlic unright in covered baking dish. Add broth. Bake 1 hour, uncover and bake 15 minutes more. Serve as side dish or use in sauces, spreads and other cooked dishes.

Spicy Roasted Potatoes

16 small red potatoes
2 tablespoons Dijon
    mustard
1 egg white
2 tablespoons vinegar
1 tablespoon paprika
1 teaspoon cumin
pinch of garlic
pinch of cayenne
pinch of black pepper
pinch of salt

SERVES 4

Preheat oven to 400°. Spray a large oven pan with 3 coats non-stick oil. Scrub potatoes, and slice into $1/_2$-inch thick rounds. Prick each round in 3-4 places with fork.

Whisk together remaining ingredients in large mixing bowl. Toss in potatoes, stir to coat. Soak potatoes in spices 15 minutes, stirring every few minutes.

Using a slotted spoon, remove potatoes and place in oven pan with some space between them. Roast in preheated oven 40 minutes, or until golden brown and tender.

Sweet Potato Pudding

3 eggs
1 cup brown sugar
pinch of salt
1¼ cups skim milk
12 oz. can skimmed
    evaporated milk
2 teaspoons soft butter
1 teaspoon nutmeg
1 teaspoon cinnamon
3½ cups raw peeled sweet
    potato, diced into
    ¼ inch cubes

Optional:
6 tablespoons raisins or
    chopped pecans

SERVES 6

Preheat oven to 325°. Spray a 2-quart baking dish with non-stick oil.

Put eggs, molasses, salt, milks, butter, nutmeg, cinnamon and 1 cup of sweet potato in blender. Process until mixture is smooth.

While blender is running, remove cover and slowly add remaining sweet potato. Pour mixture into baking dish. If desired, sprinkle raisins and/or nuts over top, and briefly stir into pudding. Bake 1 hour and 10 minutes.

THE NEW AMERICANA COOKBOOK

Curry Creamed Cauliflower and Peas

1 head cooked cauliflower
   ($2^1/_2$ cups florets)
2 cups frozen peas
2 tablespoons canola oil
2 tablespoons wheat flour
2 teaspoons curry
1 teaspoon turmeric
$^1/_2$ teaspoon ground
   cardamom
1 cup skim milk
1 tablespoon chopped
   parsley
pinch of salt
pinch of paprika

SERVES 6

Set cauliflower and peas over low heat to warm. Do not overcook.

Heat oil in a large saucepan. Blend in flour and seasonings to make a roux. Use a whisk to blend in milk. Stir until sauce is smooth and thick. Drain vegetables, add to sauce and heat together. Place in serving bowl, and sprinkle with parsley, salt and paprika.

THE NEW AMERICANA COOKBOOK

Zucchini Hash Browns

3 cups grated zucchini
1 cup grated potatoes
2 tablespoons flour
1 tablespoon grated onion
1 tablespoon chopped
    parsley
1 teaspoon black pepper
$\frac{1}{2}$ teaspoon salt
$\frac{1}{2}$ teaspoon garlic powder
1 tablespoon canola oil
2 egg whites, beaten
canola oil for frying

SERVES 4

Cover a cotton kitchen towel with paper towels. Place grated zucchini on top of paper towels. Fold towels together, twist and wring moisture out of zucchini, then measure out 3 cups. In a mixing bowl, toss zucchini and potatoes, sprinkle with flour. Stir in grated onion, parsley, and spices. Let mixture rest 15 minutes. Add 1 tablespoon canola oil and egg whites, stirring just enough to combine.

Spray large frying pan with non-stick oil. Pour in just enough oil to coat pan. Preheat pan on medium-high about 5 minutes, then fry hash browns until crispy on both sides.

In addition to its fresh uses, zucchini can be canned, pickled, or kept in the freezer up to 6 months. Cut fresh zucchini into rounds one-half inch thick. Put in individual plastic bags in the amount you will want to defrost for one meal. Place these bags in a larger plastic bag and freeze. Fresh-frozen vegetables add good flavor to cold-weather meals.

THE NEW AMERICANA COOKBOOK

Garlic Broccoli

SERVES 4

1 head broccoli
2 tablespoons olive oil
1 teaspoon lemon juice
1/4 cup white wine
pinch of salt
pinch of pepper
3-4 cloves garlic

Divide broccoli into large florets. Place on vegetable steamer over boiling water. Cover pot and steam 10 minutes, or until broccoli has just turned tender and dark green.

In a small saucepan, heat olive oil, lemon juice, wine, salt and pepper. Cut garlic cloves into quarters, add to saucepan and sauté over medium-low heat for 10 minutes. Place broccoli in serving bowl. Strain garlic sauce over broccoli.

THE NEW AMERICANA COOKBOOK

Fresh Steamed Asparagus

2 lbs. fresh asparagus

SERVES 6

Cut off bottom ends of asparagus. If stalks are thick, scrape skin off lower end. Set on steamer over boiling water, cover and steam just until tender, about 5-10 minutes.

Hollandaise Sauce

1 tablespoon cornstarch
$^3/_4$ cup water
2 tablespoons lemon juice
cayenne and salt to taste
2 egg yolks, beaten
1 tablespoon butter
1 tablespoon canola oil

Boil water in bottom of a double boiler. In top pan, whisk cornstarch with $^3/_4$ cup cold water. Add lemon juice and spices. Stirring constantly, cook until thick. Whisk in yolks, butter and oil. Stir and cook until thickened.

THE NEW AMERICANA COOKBOOK

Orange-Maple Acorn Squash

2 medium-sized acorn
   squash
8 tablespoons maple
   syrup
4 tablespoons frozen
   orange juice
   concentrate
2 teaspoons cinnamon
4 pinches of salt
boiling water

SERVES 4

Preheat oven to 375°. Cut squash lengthwise to show shape. Scoop out seeds and stringy fibers. Place in deep baking dish, open side up, so halves fit snugly into the dish.

Fill center of each squash half with 2 tablespoons maple syrup, 1 tablespoon orange juice concentrate, $1/2$ teaspoon cinnamon and a pinch of salt. Place baking dish on oven rack, then carefully pour 1 inch of boiling water in pan to surround squash. Bake 40 minutes, or until tender and golden brown.

Orange Cranberry Sauce

1 lb. fresh cranberries
1 cup orange juice
$1^1/_2$ cups brown sugar
1 teaspoon cinnamon

Wash cranberries. Cook in orange juice until their skins burst, then cook 5 minutes more. Stir in sugar and cinnamon. Serve warm, or chill to firm and use as a relish.

THE NEW AMERICANA COOKBOOK

Sweet Cider Mushroom Simmer

1 lb. fresh mushrooms
2 tablespoons safflower
   oil
1 onion, chopped
1 clove minced garlic
$\frac{1}{2}$ teaspoon oregano
sprig of fresh parsley
salt and pepper to taste
$\frac{1}{4}$ cup sweet apple cider

SERVES 5

Wash mushrooms in cold water. Slice whole mushrooms to show shape.

Sauté onion in oil until golden brown. Add mushrooms, spices and apple cider. Cover pan and cook over medium heat 15 minutes.

By 1860 most American homes had an iron cooking range instead of a searing open hearth fire. Besides ease of use and overall convenience, precision of heat became a possibility. In 1880 gas was widely available, and these stoves replaced the solid-fuel models. Electric "hot plate" stoves hit the market in 1890, but were not popular until the 1920's.

THE NEW AMERICANA COOKBOOK

Golden Onion Kuchen

3 medium-large onions
1 tablespoon butter
1 tablespoon canola oil
1 egg
8-oz. low-fat sour cream
pinch of garlic powder
pinch of salt
$1/_2$ teaspoon black pepper
1 teaspoon poppy seeds

Buttermilk Dough:
2 cups unbleached flour
1 tablespoon sugar
1 tablespoon baking
    powder
1 teaspoon baking soda
1 cup low-fat buttermilk
1 tablespoon canola oil

SERVES 6

Peel onions and slice into medium-thin rings. Heat butter and oil in a sauté pan. Add onions and sauté until they just begin to clear.

Dough: In a mixing bowl, combine dry ingredients for Buttermilk Dough. In a separate bowl, blend buttermilk and canola oil for dough. With a fork, very briefly stir buttermilk mixture into flour, just until moisetened. Spray 8-inch square baking pan with non-stick oil. Press dough into bottom of pan. Cover with sautéed onions.

In a small bowl, beat egg with sour cream, garlic powder, salt and pepper. Spoon on top of onions. Sprinkle poppy seeds over kuchen. Bake 30 minutes in 350° oven. Slice into 6 large pieces. Serve warm or cold.

Desserts
and
Sweets

THE NEW AMERICANA COOKBOOK

CONTENTS

THE NEW AMERICANA COOKBOOK

Peach Melba Cobbler

10 ripe peaches
1 pint raspberries
$^3/_4$ cup + 4 tablespoons
    sugar
1 tablespoon quick
    tapioca
1 tablespoon fresh lemon
    juice
2 cups all-purpose flour
pinch of salt
1 tablespoon baking
    powder
3 tablespoons canola oil
2 tablespoons butter
1 teaspoon vanilla
1 egg
$^1/_2$ cup skim milk

SERVES 8

Preheat oven to 400°. Spray a large casserole or baking dish with non-stick oil.

Poach peaches in boiling water for 3 minutes. Remove, cool and peel off skin. Slice peaches into thin crescents. In a mixing bowl combine peaches, raspberries, $^3/_4$-cup sugar, tapioca and lemon juice. Spread in baking dish.

Combine flour, salt, baking powder, oil, butter, vanilla and 2 tablespoons sugar with a pastry cutter or fingertips until mixture resembles small peas. In a separate bowl, beat together egg and milk, then stir into flour mixture. Knead lightly in bowl. Break off pieces of dough and gently press over fruit to form a "cobbled" topping. Sprinkle with remaining 2 tablespoons sugar. Bake 35-40 minutes or until golden brown. Serve warm.

Deep Dish Apple-Cranberry Crisp

*For the best flavor, use McIntosh, Jonathan, Golden Delicious
or other good-cooking apple varieties.*

SERVES 8

8 ripe apples, peeled,
   cored and cut into
   $1/4$-inch thick slices
1 tablespoon lemon juice
1 teaspoon quick tapioca
$1^{1}/_{4}$ cups cranberries
$1^{1}/_{2}$ cups brown sugar
$1^{1}/_{4}$ cups golden raisins
2 teaspoons cinnamon
2 teaspoons finely grated
   lemon rind
1 teaspoon vanilla extract
2 cups unbleached flour
1 tablespoon baking
   powder
3 tablespoons sugar
2 tablespoons canola oil
1 egg, beaten
$1/3$ cup skim milk
$1/4$ cup ice water
1 tablespoon sugar mixed
   1 teaspoon cinnamon

Preheat oven to 425°. Spray a 3-quart casserole or soufflé dish with non-stick oil.

In a large mixing bowl sprinkle lemon juice and tapioca over apple slices, toss. In a separate bowl, pound cranberries until at least half been crushed. Stir in brown sugar. Mix cranberries, raisins, lemon rind and vanilla into apples. Pour in to prepared baking dish.

Combine flour, baking powder and sugar. In a separate bowl combine oil, egg, milk and water. Make a well in middle of flour and pour in liquid mixture. Use a fork to distribute liquid and stir in to dough. Roll between sheets of wax paper. Slice dough into $1/2$-inch strips. Weave strips in a tight lattice pattern over fruit. Sprinkle top of crisp with cinnamon and sugar. Bake in preheated oven 40-45 minutes. Serve hot.

THE NEW AMERICANA COOKBOOK

Key Lime Pie

*The Key lime is a native of Florida. Its uniquely
fresh lime flavor has made this pie famous.*

Pie Shell:

1$\frac{1}{2}$ cups crushed graham
    cracker squares
$\frac{1}{4}$ cup packed brown
    sugar
1 tablespoon lime juice
1 tablespoon softened
    butter

Filling:

15-oz. can non-fat
    evaporated milk
1 tablespoon grated Key
    lime rind
$\frac{1}{2}$ cup Key lime juice
1 teaspoon vanilla
$\frac{1}{2}$ cup sugar
1 egg yolk, beaten

Meringue:

2 egg whites
2 tablespoons sugar

SERVES 6

In a mixing bowl, combine pie shell ingredients with a fork, distributing moisture evenly. Press into a 9-inch pie shell that has been sprayed with non-stick oil.

Preheat oven to 350°. Stir together filling ingredients until thickened. (The lime juice will react with the milk to thicken it.) Pour into pie shell.

Beat egg whites, slowly adding sugar, until stiff. Cover filling with meringue.

Bake 15 minutes, or until meringue is lightly browned on the peaks. Chill before serving.

THE NEW AMERICANA COOKBOOK

Blue Ribbon Blueberry Pie

Crust:
2½ cups all-purpose flour
3 tablespoons sugar
½ cup canola oil
5 tablespoons ice water
1 tablespoon skim milk

Blueberry Filling:
4 cups wild blueberries
⅓ cup sugar
⅓ cup brown sugar
1 tablespoon quick
    tapioca
½ teaspoon cinnamon
½ teaspoon nutmeg
1 tablespoon lemon juice

Glaze:
1 tablespoon skim milk
1 tablespoon sugar

MAKES 9-INCH PIE

Preheat oven to 400°. Spray 9-inch pie plate with non-stick oil.

Crust: Combine flour and sugar. With pastry cutter or knives, cut oil into mixture. Use fork to blend in water and milk. Divide dough in half, and roll each between two sheets of wax paper. Place bottom crust in pie plate.

Clean fresh blueberries (if canned or frozen set to drain) and put in bowl. In a separate bowl, mix sugars, tapioca, cinnamon and nutmeg. Sprinkle lemon juice on blueberries, then gently fold into sugar mixture. Let sit 45 minutes, then gently stir again. Pour into pie shell. Cover with second crust. Crimp edges with fingers and flute. Make 5 small slits in top. Brush top with milk and sprinkle with sugar. Bake 10 minutes at 400°, reduce heat to 350° and bake 25 minutes more.

THE NEW AMERICANA COOKBOOK

Perfect Pumpkin Pie

*This custardy filling also bakes well in cups for a light desert.
And don't forget the fat-free whipped cream topping!*

Pie Crust:
1¹/₃ cups all-purpose flour
2 tablespoons sugar
6 tablespoons canola oil
4 tablespoons skim milk

Pumpkin Filling:
2 cups pumpkin purée
2 tablespoons melted
  butter
³/₄ cup brown sugar
¹/₂ teaspoon nutmeg
pinch of cloves
³/₄ cup skimmed
  evaporated milk
2 eggs, separated
1 tablespoon sugar

MAKES ONE 9-INCH PIE

Pie Crust: Sift flour and sugar together. In a separate bowl, combine oil and milk, and pour into flour. Blend with a fork and roll into a ball. If too dry to hold together, add a little milk. Wrap in plastic, chill 15 minutes. Roll dough between sheets of wax paper. Place in pie dish sprayed with non-stick oil.

Pumpkin Filling: Preheat oven to 400°. Beat together filling ingredients, except egg whites and tablespoon sugar. Beat together the egg whites and sugar until stiff, then gently fold into pumpkin. Pour into crust, flute and trim. Bake 50 minutes or until toothpick inserted in center comes out clean.

Fresh pumpkin purée: preheat oven to 400°. Cut top off pumpkin and remove seeds. Line baking pan with tin-foil. Replace top of pumpkin. Bake on pan until very soft, about two hours. Remove pan from oven and cool before scooping out pulp. Let pulp set and liquid will separate, drain off. Purée in blender. Let set, again, drain off separated liquid.

THE NEW AMERICANA COOKBOOK

Fruity California Cookies

*These easy drop cookies use your favorite dried fruits and nuts,
which all grow in our most famous agricultural state.*

1 cup quick-cooking
    rolled oats
1 cup unbleached flour
$1/2$ teaspoon cinnamon
$1/2$ teaspoon baking soda
3 tablespoons softened
    butter
2 tablespoons canola oil
1 cup light brown sugar
1 egg
1 teaspoon vanilla or
    almond extract
1 cup chopped dried
    fruits and nuts

MAKES 4 DOZEN COOKIES

Preheat oven to 350°. Spray cookie sheets with non-stick oil.

In a mixing bowl, combine oats, flour, cinnamon and baking soda. In a separate bowl, cream the butter, oil, brown sugar, egg, and vanilla or almond extract. Beat the dry ingredients into the creamed mixture. Stir in the chopped fruits and nuts by hand.

Use 2 teaspoons to drop rounded teaspoons of batter onto the cookie sheet, about 2 inches apart. Bake 10 minutes, or just until light gold. Allow cookies to cool for 1 minute on cookie sheet, then transfer to wire racks.

THE NEW AMERICANA COOKBOOK

A Summer's Night Chocolate Kisses

4 egg whites
pinch of salt
$^1/_4$ teaspoon cream of
 tartar
$^1/_3$ cup granulated sugar
$^1/_2$ cup confectioner's
 sugar
3 tablespoons cocoa
 powder

MAKES FORTY 1-INCH MERINGUES

Preheat oven to 200°. Spray cookie sheet with non-stick oil.

Beat egg whites with salt and cream of tartar until foamy. Slowly beat in granulated sugar, 1 tablespoon at a time (the meringue should become stiff.) Using a spatula, gently fold in confections's sugar and cocoa.

Drop by the teaspoon onto cookie sheet and shape into cones. Bake 25-30 minutes, or until outsides are firm to the touch and insides are still soft. These kisses are very fragile, so handle with TLC until cool!

THE NEW AMERICANA COOKBOOK

Praline Cookies
These sweet treats have a candy crunch!

1$\frac{1}{2}$ cups flour
$\frac{1}{4}$ teaspoon ground
    ginger
dash of salt
1 cup packed brown sugar
1 cup sugar
2 tablespoons butter
1 teaspoon vanilla extract
1 tablespoon skim milk
1 tablespoon water
$\frac{3}{4}$ cup ground pecans

MAKES 48 PRALINES

Preheat oven to 350°. Spray a cookie sheet with non-stick oil. Sift flour, ginger and salt.

In a 1 quart pot over medium-low heat, combine sugars and stir frequently until completely melted. Blend in butter, vanilla, milk, and water. Reduce heat to low. Gradually stir in flour mixture, then pecans.

Soak 2 teaspoons in cup of hot water. With mixture on stove, use spoons to place by the teaspoon onto sheet. Dip teaspoons in hot water as needed. Bake 7-8 minutes. Let cool 5 minutes on cookie sheet, then transfer to ceramic plate sprayed with non-stick oil.

THE NEW AMERICANA COOKBOOK

Gingerbread People

My niece, Amanda, would be truly distraught if "Gingerbread" were an exclusive men's club.

$^1/_4$ cup canola oil
$^1/_2$ cup sugar
$^1/_2$ cup dark molasses
$3^1/_2$ cups all-purpose flour
1 teaspoon baking soda
$^1/_4$ teaspoon cloves
$^1/_2$ teaspoon cinnamon
2 teaspoons ginger
pinch of salt
$^1/_4$ cup water

MAKES EIGHT 5-INCH LONG PEOPLE

Preheat oven to 350°. Spray cookie sheet with non-stick oil.

Using electric beater, blend oil, sugar and molasses. Sift flour, then resift with remaining dry ingredients. Mix flour mixture into wet mixture in three parts, alternating each addition with one-third of the water. Roll dough on a lightly floured surface, about $^1/_4$ inch thick. Cut out gingerbread people with cookie cutter or knife. Set on cookie sheet. Use raisins or candied fruits for features and buttons. Bake until dough springs back when lightly pressed, about 8-10 minutes.

Decorating Gingerbread People: For each icing color, blend together $^1/_4$ cup confectioner's sugar, a few drops of vanilla, water, and 1-2 drops food coloring into a paste. Apply icing with a small knife. To add detail and texture, use a wooden toothpick. (This recipe can also be used to construct Gingerbread Houses.)

THE NEW AMERICANA COOKBOOK

Maple Curls

1 cup maple syrup
$^1/_2$ cup canola oil
1 cup all-purpose flour
pinch of salt

MAKES THIRTY 3-INCH CURLS

Preheat oven to 350°. Spray cookie sheet with non-stick oil.

Boil maple syrup and oil together for 30 seconds. Remove from heat, stir in flour and salt until well blended.

Drop dough by the tablespoon onto cookie sheet, leaving 3 inches between them. Bake 9-12 minutes, until cookie is the color of maple syrup. Remove pan from oven and let cool 1 minute, then remove cookies one at a time. Place handle of wooden spoon on edge of cookie and roll into a curl around handle.

THE NEW AMERICANA COOKBOOK

Berry Cream Custard

1 cup frozen berries
   (strawberries,
   raspberries or
   blueberries)
2 cups skim milk
³/₄ cup honey
pinch of salt
2 beaten eggs
¹/₂ teaspoon vanilla
¹/₂ cup sugar

SERVES 4

Preheat oven to 300°. Spray 5 individual custard cups with non-stick oil.

Set berries to drain in sieve and reserve juice. In a saucepan on medium heat, blend milk, honey and salt, and scald milk. Remove from heat, whisk in eggs and vanilla. Pour custard filling into prepared cups. Place cups in deep-dish baking pan, then fill baking pan with 1¹/₂ inches of very hot (not boiling) water. Bake 50 minutes. Chill custard cups.

Boil reserved berry juice with sugar for 10 minutes. Remove from heat, stir in berries. Spoon berry sauce over cooled custard cups.

THE NEW AMERICANA COOKBOOK

Indian Corn Pudding

4 cups skim milk
$^2/_3$ cup yellow cornmeal
pinch of salt
$^1/_2$ cup molasses or sugar
2 teaspoons cinnamon
1 egg
$^1/_2$ cup cold milk

SERVES 8

Preheat oven to 325°. Spray a 2-quart baking dish with non-stick oil.

Scald 4 cups milk. Stir milk while slowly adding cornmeal, salt, molasses or sugar, and cinnamon. Remove from heat.

Beat egg, then whisk into mixture. Pour into casserole, bake 1 hour. Pour one-half cup cold milk over top of pudding, without stirring, and bake another $1^1/_2$-2 hours. Serve pudding hot with a topping of non-fat whipped cream or frozen yogurt.

Instead of expanding the spice chests of Europe, Columbus' journey to the New World introduced corn to northern Spain, Portugal and Italy, where it became a staple part of the diet. The discovery of the Americas also brought the Europeans potatoes, chocolate, peanuts, vanilla, tomatoes, pineapples, lima beans, peppers, tapioca and turkey.

THE NEW AMERICANA COOKBOOK

Lemon Cheesecake

Cheesecake Crust:
2 cups sugared graham
    cracker crumbs
2 tablespoons canola oil
1 tablespoon lemon juice

Cheesecake Filling:
3 eggs
16 oz. light cream cheese,
    softened
16 oz. non-fat sour cream
$1/2$ cup part-skim Ricotta
    cheese, well drained
2 tablespoons cornstarch
$1^{1}/_{2}$ cups sugar
2 tablespoons lemon juice
1 teaspoon finely grated
    lemon rind
2 teaspoons vanilla extract
pinch of salt

MAKES 9-INCH CHEESECAKE

Combine crust ingredients in mixing bowl. Spray 9-inch spring-mold pan with non-stick oil. Press crust mixture into bottom of pan and $2^{1}/_{2}$ inches up the sides. Bake in 375° oven 3 minutes, then chill.

In blender, whip eggs, cream cheese, sour cream, Ricotta cheese and cornstarch. Pour into mixing bowl and stir in remaining ingredients. Beat until completely smooth. Pour into crust and bake at 325° until just set, about 50 minutes. Turn off oven, leaving cheesecake inside, for 1 hour more. Cool completely at room temperature, then chill at least 6 hours before serving. Garnish with fresh fruit.

Frosted Pear Spice Cake

1 1/2 cups packed brown
    sugar
1/2 cup safflower oil
1 cup applesauce
1 teaspoon vanilla
2 teaspoons baking
    powder
1/2 teaspoon baking soda
2 teaspoons cinnamon
1 teaspoon ginger
1 teaspoon cloves
2 1/2 cups all-purpose flour
3 eggs
3 medium-size ripe pears
1/2 cup chopped almonds

Frosting:
2 tablespoons skim milk
8 oz. non-fat cream
    cheese
1 teaspoon vanilla
2 1/2 cups confectioner's
    sugar

SERVES 12

Preheat oven to 350°. Spray a 9" x 13" baking pan with non-stick oil.

With electric beater, combine sugar, oil, applesauce, vanilla, baking powder, baking soda, cinnamon, ginger, cloves, salt and flour. Beat at medium-high speed 5 minutes. Add eggs, beating after each one.

Peel pears and chop into very small pieces. With a rubber spatula, fold pears and nuts into batter. Spread batter in baking pan. Bake 50 minutes, or until toothpick inserted in center comes out clean. Remove cake from pan, and cool on wire rack before frosting.

Frosting: Combine milk, cream cheese and vanilla with electric beater until fluffy. Slowly add sugar until frosting is of spreading consistency. Frost when cake is cool.

Seasonal Preserves & Jams

THE NEW AMERICANA COOKBOOK

CONTENTS

ABOUT CANNING

Jars: Use only properly sealed canning jars with rubber airtight seals or a two-piece metal screw-down lid. Check against defects such as chips or cracks. Jars must be sterilized in boiling water or dishwasher, and filled while still hot.

Packing Jars: Fill while preserves and jar are very hot, leaving $1/4$ to $1/2$-inch headroom. Before sealing, release trapped air by running a butter knife or spatula down the insides of the jar. Wipe top of jar clean before sealing.

Canning at a High Altitude: Increase processing time in boiling water bath by 1 minute for every 1000 feet above sea level.

THE NEW AMERICANA COOKBOOK

Citrus Marmalade

1 large grapefruit
3 large oranges
2 lemons
10 cups water
7 cups sugar

MAKES ABOUT 16 JELLY JARS

Scrub fruit well. Halve and discard seeds. Scoop pulp into saucepan, then grate in the rind. Add water and let set for 12 hours.

Boil fruit and water mixture for 20 minutes. Refrigerate another 12 hours.

Return to stove and warm mixture on low heat. Add sugar and stir until dissolved. Raise heat to moderate, and cook until 222° is reached on a candy thermometer.

Pour into hot sterilized jars. Seal jars according to manufacturer's directions.

THE NEW AMERICANA COOKBOOK

Cherry Jam

3 lbs. ripe cherries
1 cup water
1 cup orange juice
1 tablespoon lemon juice
3 cups sugar

MAKES 4 PINTS
Read about canning on page 150.

Cut cherries into quarters and discard pits. Bring cherries, water and juices to a full boil. Simmer for 20 minutes. Stir in sugar until completely dissolved. Taste, add sugar or lemon juice as desired. Continue stirring and simmer 30 minutes. Pour into hot jars, seal.

Place jars on rack in boiler half-filled with boiling water, leaving space between jars. Add boiling water to cover jars 2 inches above their tops. Bring to a boil, cover, and process 10 minutes. Using tongs, lift jars (not by the lids) and set on towels with several inches between them to cool.

An herbal cough syrup: Pour 1 cup boiling water over 2 tablespoons of dried sweet cicely and steep for 30 minutes. Combine 2 tablespoons of this tea with 2 tablespoons honey and 1 tablespoon lemon juice.

THE NEW AMERICANA COOKBOOK

Great Grape Jelly

4 cups crushed Concord
    grapes, preferably
    slightly underripe
$1/2$ cup water
1 apple, cut in quarters
1 tablespoon cider vinegar
sugar
1 pouch (3 oz.) liquid
    fruit pectin

MAKES ABOUT 4 CUPS

Put crushed grapes in large pan and add water, apple quarters and vinegar. Boil 20 minutes, stirring occasionally. Skim froth. Remove from heat. Strain through jelly bag or very fine sieve. Discard skins and seeds.

Measure grape juice. To each cup of juice add three-quarters cup sugar. Stir well to dissolve. Mix in liquid pectin, then return to pan and boil, uncovered, for 3 minutes. Skim off froth. Pour into hot sterilized jars. Seal according to manufacturer's directions.

THE NEW AMERICANA COOKBOOK

Hot Pepper Jelly

MAKES 3 JELLY JARS

1 cup finely chopped
    green pepper
1-2 finely chopped
    jalapeno peppers
3/4 cup cider vinegar
2 cups sugar
1 teaspoon white pepper
3 oz. liquid pectin

Purée both peppers and vinegar in blender or food processor until smooth. Pour into saucepan and stir in sugar and white pepper. Bring to a full boil. Remove from heat. Rest for 5 minutes, then skim off foam. Add pectin and pour into hot sterilized jelly jars.

Will keep in refrigerator 2 weeks. You can also process as jelly and seal with paraffin or a two-piece metal screw-down lid, according to manufacturer's instructions.

When working with hot peppers, remember they contain oils that can cause painful burns to sensitive skin. Do not rub your eyes, nose, mouth, or face before throughly washing your hands. Also, childrens' skin is especially delicate and can be hurt by hot pepper oils. Some cooks prefer to wear rubber gloves to work with hot peppers and seeds.

THE NEW AMERICANA COOKBOOK

Lemon Curd

My favorite spread on toast, biscuits or waffles.
Contains only 1 gram of fat per teaspoon. Enjoy!

1 cup sugar
3 eggs
2 egg yolks
$^3/_8$ cup lemon juice
1 teaspoon cornstarch
4 tablespoons melted
    butter
4 tablespoons finely
    grated lemon rind

MAKES $1^1/_2$ CUPS

Combine sugar, eggs and egg yolks in a small bowl. Beat with electric beater for 2 minutes, then beat in lemon juice and cornstarch.

Pour mixture into saucepan. Cook over medium heat, stirring constantly, for 10 minutes or until thickened.

Return cooked mixture to bowl and beat briefly. Continue to beat while gradually adding melted butter and grated lemon rind. Place curd into jars and cover with plastic. Chill and store in refrigerator, where curd will firm. Lemon curd will keep about a month.

THE NEW AMERICANA COOKBOOK

Yankee Piccalli Preserves

1 peck green tomatoes,
  diced
12 onions, diced
$^3/_4$ cup pickling salt
3 quarts cider vinegar
12 green peppers, diced
6 sweet red peppers, diced
10 cloves garlic, minced
1 lb. light brown sugar
4 cups honey
2 tablespoons mustard
2 tablespoons ground
  cloves
2 tablespoons cinnamon
2 tablespoons ginger
1 tablespoon celery seed

MAKES 12 PINTS
Read about canning on page 150.

Toss tomatoes and onions with salt. Refrigerate 12 hours, then rinse and drain. Boil remaining ingredients, add tomatoes and onions. Simmer 1 hour. Pack in hot sterilized jars leaving $^1/_2$ inch headroom. Seal.

Place jars on rack in boiler half-filled with boiling water, leaving space between jars. Add boiling water to cover jars 2 inches above their tops. Boil, cover, and process 15 minutes. Using tongs, lift jars (not by the lids) and set on towels, with a space between them, to cool.

Pickled Beets

2 lbs. peeled and thinly
    sliced beets
2 quarts water
2 tablespoons pickling
    salt
1$\frac{1}{2}$ cups vinegar
1$\frac{1}{2}$ cups water
1 cup sugar
1 teaspoon peppercorns
1 teaspoon mustard seed

MAKES 4 PINTS
Read about canning on page 150.

Boil beets 10 minutes in 2 quarts water with pickling salts. Drain and pack in sterilized jars. Boil all other ingredients together, and simmer for 3 minutes. Pour hot liquid over beets, leaving $\frac{1}{2}$-inch headroom, seal.

Place jars on rack in boiler half-filled with boiling water, leaving space between jars. Add boiling water to cover jars 2 inches above their tops. Bring to a boil, cover and process 10 minutes. Using tongs, lift jars (not by the lids) and set on towels with several inches between them to cool.

By around 10,000 B.C., in the Near East and Asia, men had specialized their knowledge in the ways of animals, and women in the ways of plants. The historical record indicates these women were the first farmers, who studied and cultivated the natural tendencies of plants and their propagational preferences.

THE NEW AMERICANA COOKBOOK

Sweet & Sour Pickles

5 lbs. small pickling
   cucumbers, scrubbed
$1/4$ cup pickling salt
boiling water
3 cups water
4 cups cider vinegar
2 cups sugar
2 tablespoons whole
   mixed pickling spices
6-inches broken
   cinnamon sticks
1 teaspoon whole cloves

MAKES 6 PINTS
Read about canning on page 150.

Cover cucumbers with cold water mixed with pickling salt. Soak 24 hours, then drain. Briefly cover cucumbers with boiling water, drain, then pack into sterilized jars. Boil 3 cups water with remaining ingredients. Fill jars with boiling vinegar mixture. Seal jars.

Place jars on rack in boiler half-filled with boiling water, leaving space between jars. Add boiling water to cover jars 2 inches above their tops. Boil, cover, and process 15 minutes. Use tongs to lift jars, set on towels with several inches between them to cool.

THE NEW AMERICANA COOKBOOK

Curried Apricot Chutney

2 cups water
2 cups chopped dried
    apricots
$\frac{1}{2}$ cup onion, chopped
    fine
$\frac{1}{2}$ cup sugar
$1\frac{1}{2}$ cups cider vinegar
1 teaspoon ginger
2 teaspoons curry powder
1 teaspoon cinnamon
pinch of salt
1 cup golden raisins

MAKES 2 PINTS
Read about canning on page 150.

Simmer water, apricots, onions and sugar 30 minutes. In a separate pan, cook vinegar and spices over medium heat for 5 minutes. Combine both mixtures with raisins. Pack in hot sterilized jars and seal.

Place jars on rack in boiler half-filled with boiling water, leaving space between jars. Add boiling water to cover jars 2 inches above their tops. Bring to a boil, cover and process 10 minutes. Using tongs, lift jars (not by the lids) and set on towels with several inches between them to cool.

THE NEW AMERICANA COOKBOOK

Notes on Using This Cookbook

The New Americana Cookbook, A Heart-Healthy Excursion Through Regional Cuisines, has been written to take advantage of the diversity of fresh produce. Try to buy locally grown produce in the freshest condition possible. Your foods will then provide the most flavor and vitamins, and also be the most economical.

To allow for a diversity of foods, fruits and vegetables which freeze or dry well are also used in their preferred state of storage.

Non-fat and low-fat dairy products are readily available, and provide calcium, protein, nutrition and flavor, with much less fat. They are incorporated into these recipes and are an excellent substitute to whole milk products.

Fresh produce, fish, grains, flours, dairy and beans provide a diverse and healthy diet, without the animal fats and other problems associated with meat.

Non-stick oil spray is intended to mean a non-fat vegetable oil spray. When used in combination with a cooking oil, it allows the use of less oil.

Preheating the oven or broiler takes only 15 minutes. Save electricity: don't warm your appliances until 15 minutes before they will be used.

THE NEW AMERICANA COOKBOOK

Following the Guidelines of The American Heart Association

A complete statement of the Guidelines of the American Heart Association can be obtained by contacting your local chapter. For healthy adults, this cookbook presents a common-sense approach to following these guidelines without the detailed weighing and measuring of each food item.

By deleting most meat, a large amount of saturated fat (an artery-damaging fat) will be replaced by more healthful protein and fats. Saturated fats should be limited to 10% of calories. All animal products, including chicken and cheese, also contain cholesterol, and their use should be limited.

Polyunsaturated fat (found in salmon, leafy vegetables and seeds) will reduce cholesterol in the blood. Polyunsaturated Omega-3 fatty acids are believed to have an anticlotting agent, and assist in preventing heart attack and stroke.

Monounsaturated fats also reduce the damaging LDL cholesterol, and are found in olive and canola oils.

Total fat intake should not exceed 25-30% of the calories consumed. Even polyunsaturated and monounsaturated fats should be consumed in limited quantities, and will achieve the greatest results if they replace, not supplement, the saturated fats presently consumed.

THE NEW AMERICANA COOKBOOK

Following the Guidelines of
The American Heart Association

(cont.) Carbohydrates should make up at least 50-60% of the diet. This includes vegetables, fruits, grains, flours and beans. The American Heart Association recommends calories be adjusted to achieve and maintian a healthy body weight.

Make a habit of reaching for fruit or naturally sweetened products. The recipes in this book offer a reasonable alternative to the traditional high-fat and caloric desserts, but they are not intended to be eaten everyday, or in volumes greater than those proportionately shown as a serving.

It is critical that the volume of prepared food products be kept to reasonable proportions. In this way, a wide variety of foods can be enjoyed, and you will benefit from a broad range of the natural vitamins, minerals and nutrients. Fresh fruits and vegetables may be eaten regularly, without restriction.

Salt intake should follow the advise of your physician, or be limited to 3 grams per day. Recipes in this book can be made without salt or allow for "salt to taste." The desire for salty foods is acquired, you can become more sensitive to the taste of salt by slowly reducing its volume.   Try using sea salt in small amounts, it is more flavorful and contains minerals not present in table salt.

Alcohol consumption should not exceed 1-2 drinks per day.   And...
Exercise! It makes your body work better, and feel better, too.

THE NEW AMERICANA COOKBOOK

Suggested Kitchen Tools, Utensils and Stock Items

Kitchen Tools and Utensils:
Set of whisks in assorted sizes
Slotted spoon and spatula
Blender
Double boiler
Non-stick skillet and frying pans in assorted sizes with lids
Oven casseroles with lids
Non-aluminum pots, pans and containers
Rolling pin
Large stainless steel bowl for mixing bread doughs
Pie pans, regular and deep-dish

Stock Items:
A good variety of spices, fresh fruits and vegetables
Non-stick, non-fat vegetable oil spray
Canola, olive and safflower oils
Vegetable bouillon cubes or powder
Skim milk
Non-fat powdered milk (to enrich skim milk)
Low-fat buttermilk
Non-fat plain yogurt, cottage cheese and cream cheese

THE NEW AMERICANA COOKBOOK

Measurements

a pinch..................................... $^1/_8$ teaspoon or less
3 teaspoons............................... 1 tablespoon

4 tablespoons........................... $^1/_4$ cup
16 tablespoons........................ 1 cup
2 cups..................................... 1 pint
4 cups..................................... 1 quart
4 quarts.................................. 1 gallon
8 quarts.................................. 1 peck
16 ounces................................ 1 pound
8 ounces liquid....................... 1 cup
1 ounce liquid......................... 2 tablespoons

Substitutions

1 tablespoon cornstarch............ 2 T. flour or 2 tsp. quick-cooking tapioca
2 teaspoons arrowroot.............. 1 tablespoon cornstarch
1 teaspoon baking powder.......... $^1/_4$ tsp. baking soda + $^1/_2$ tsp. cream of tartar
$^1/_2$ cup brown sugar.................. 2 T. molasses in $^1/_2$ cup granulated sugar
$^3/_4$ cup cracker crumbs.............. 1 cup bread crumbs
1 tablespoon fresh herbs........... 1 teaspoon dried herbs
1 small clove garlic.................. $^1/_8$ teaspoon garlic powder
1 fresh onion.......................... 2 T. instant minced onion, rehydrated
1 cup whole milk..................... $^1/_2$ c. skimmed evaporated milk + $^1/_2$ c. water
1 cup buttermilk...................... 1 cup non-fat plain yogurt

THE NEW AMERICANA COOKBOOK

THE NEW AMERICANA COOKBOOK

THE NEW AMERICANA COOKBOOK

THE NEW AMERICANA COOKBOOK

THE NEW AMERICANA COOKBOOK

PRINTED IN THE U.S.A.
ON ACID FREE PAPER